AWAKE
A New Beginning

AWAKE
A New Beginning

Rhonda Reneé Durand

Word Association Publishers
205 Fifth Avenue
Tarentum, Pennsylvania 15084

Copyright© 2006 by Rhonda R. Durand

All rights reserved. No part of this book may be used or reproduced in any manner whatsoever without written permission of the author.

Printed in the United States of America.

ISBN 10: 1-59571-132-5
ISBN 13: 978-1-59571-132-8
Library of Congress Control Number: 2006927269

Word Association Publishers
205 Fifth Avenue
Tarentum, Pennsylvania 15084
www.wordassociation.com
1-800-827-7903

*First, I thank God for a second chance.
Next I thank my mom, brothers, and the many doctors, nurses, therapists and praying people involved in my recovery process.
I thank you all from the bottom of my heart.*

"Our God is an awesome God!"

*In loving memory of Pastor Russ Nelson.
Our best friend and mentor.*

Jesus replied, "you do not realize what I am doing now, but later you will understand." - John.13:7

November 19, 1986
LAKELAND RESIDENTS HURT IN CRASH

LAKELAND - Two Lakeland residents received serious injuries Tuesday night when their cars collided on West Pipkin Road, about five miles south of Lakeland.

The driver of a 1976 Pontiac identified as Rhonda R. Dzurovcin 19, of 18 Noel Drive, was in critical condition Tuesday night at Lakeland Regional Medical Center, according to the patrol.

Dzurovcin's car was traveling west on Pipkin Road about 7:20 p.m. when it started to make a U-turn and was struck on the driver's side by a second westbound car, according to the patrol. The driver of the second car, was taken to Lakeland Regional in serious condition.

No charges were filed Tuesday in connection with the accident.

"I went down to the bottom of the mountains, the earth with her bars were about me forever, yet thou hast brought me up from corruption, oh lord my God, while I was fainting away, I remembered the Lord and my prayers came to thee into thy holy temple!" - Jonah 2:6 & 7

Seventy-two hours left to live

THE EVENING WAS like any other for my mother and brother. Mom was getting ready to report for the midnight shift at Allegheny Ludlum Steel Company in Brackenridge, Pennsylvania and my brother was doing his homework. I had been living away from home for the past seventeen months. I had impulsively run off to Florida with a young man I had only known for three months—a man my mother had forbidden me to see—the man who was now my fiancé.

The phone rang and my mother answered. It was a doctor from the Lakeland, Florida hospital calling to notify my mother that her nineteen-year-old daughter had been involved in a serious accident. Mom's heart raced as he told her that my body had suffered a great trauma—so great that I had begun to revert to the fetal position.

"According to statistics," he said, "she will be brain dead in seventy-two hours, even though she's on life support now."

Mom shook as she told Dom what happened. She watched in stunned silence, as he walked into the bathroom horrifying her with his screams and sobbing.

She banged and banged on the door and finally, when he opened it, with tears streaming down his face, he told her "I don't want to lose my sister. What if Rhonda dies?"

Mom then phoned my older brother, Dean who was in Pensacola, Florida in the service. And as Dean prepared to race the distance from Pensacola to Lakeland, Mom and Dom made plane reservations on the first flight out of Pittsburgh.

Dean made the eight hour trip in seven hours and my Mother and Dom arrived the next day. They all kept watching the machines that I was hooked-up to, not knowing what the next hour would bring.

When Dean got to the hospital doctors explained that I had a broken pelvis, clavicle and, worst of all, a twisted brain stem and a severe, closed head injury, known as a T.B.I. (traumatic brain injury) Being a medical technician in the Air Force, Dean understood all too well the severity of my situation.

But it wasn't until the next day when Mom and Dom joined

AWAKE

Dean and my boyfriend, Dan at the hospital that they noticed my body was covered with bruises from head to toe. When Mom commented on this to the doctor he said,

"I was thinking that Rhonda's got entirely too many bruises for all of them to have come from the car accident alone."

Dan had been the first to arrive at the hospital, doing a good job of portraying the distraught boyfriend. But following her conversation with the doctor, Mom immediately began questioning Dan about the multitude of bruises on my body. Dan suddenly erupted in anger and actually threatened to hit Mom if she didn't stop. In a moment, he was escorted from the hospital and Mom made certain he was never allowed back.

My Mother and brothers wasted no time in going to the trailer where Dan and I lived to get my belongings. But to their surprise, Dan had already taken everything—his clothes, my clothes and all of our personal items. While there, my next door neighbor and her young granddaughter came over. Both were crying as they told my family about the horrific beating that I had suffered just two days before the crash.

"I thought he was going to kill her. She was screaming and their trailer was bouncing from one end to the other." P.J. told my horrified mother and brothers.

"I walked into their trailer, held a baseball bat over Dan's head and yelled for Rhonda to run."

It was clear to my family that P.J. had saved my life which made the subsequent car crash all the more unbearable for them.

P.J.'s granddaughter, little Anna, who was not more than six at the time, gave my Mother an angel pin.

"Here," she said through her tears, "give this to Rhonda to help her get better."

Mom took that white angel pin and pinned it to my pillow and through my years of recovery and hospital stays, the angel never left my side.

One of my prayers today is that little Anna has been blessed as much as I have. I ask God to bless her with love, peace, and happiness. Her compassion meant so much to me.

Mom, Dom and Dean would spend the first few days sleeping in the waiting room outside of the Intensive Care Unit.

My dad, however, would remain in Pennsylvania. He

never lived with us. He never had anything to do with us. When my uncle phoned him to tell him about my accident and that I was near death, my dad had nothing to say.

"Ron, wouldn't you like to go to Rhonda, to be by her side at this terrible time? She has only been given seventy-two hours to live."

But Ron explained that he was much too busy with his business to make the trip.

Meanwhile, Mom prayed to God, "Please be with her. Please take care of her. Please!"

It must have seemed that God wasn't listening because my doctor soon advised my Mother to begin making funeral arrangements. He told her that, according to statistics, he was certain I didn't have long.

Mom was naturally overwhelmed. She was terrified, exhausted and couldn't eat. One day she collapsed. The doctors who examined her thought that it was her heart and advised her to follow-up with a cardiologist when she got home. My brothers urged her to try to rest and eat so that she would be strong for me and she was soon able to maintain her vigil at my bedside.

We had never been a religious family. We never went to church but I will be forever grateful that my Mother had the wisdom to pray right from the start and never give up on God. Mom even asked for prayers from strangers at airports and on the planes. I'm certain that every single prayer reached His holy throne of grace. Don't ever give up on prayer!

When Mom searched for hope from other doctors who were taking care of me, she got little comfort.

"If she comes out of it (and it's a big if) she might not be much more than a vegetable," one Doctor had told my family. "At best, she'll be terribly impaired—not able to talk or walk—not ever."

The seventy-two hours turned into days and the days turned into weeks. Still the doctors offered little hope. My family waited and watched. They were told not to cry or talk about my dire situation when they were in the room. The common belief is that coma patients, even those who are dying, may be able to hear.

Many times, Mom would run to the rest room to sob. One

day, while she was crying, she felt a tap on her shoulder and turned around.

The young woman standing there, Mom noticed, was small and thin and had beautiful, dark hair and a soft, warm smile. " She looks a lot like Rhonda," thought Mom.

"Why are you crying?" the girl asked.

"It's my daughter," Mom sobbed. "She's been in an automobile accident."

"Yes, I know," the young girl said.

Mom went on. "She's in a coma."

The girl looked at Mom confidently and said "Well, you KNOW that she'll pull through this, don't you?"

Then she put her hand on Mom's shoulder and said, "Trust me, she will be all right."

Taken by the girl's kindness and her uncanny resemblance to her daughter, Mom thanked her for the encouragement and kindness and then asked the girl's name.

"Rhonda," she said, "My name is Rhonda."

With that, Mom reached for another tissue and when she looked back, the girl was gone. But Mom had never heard a sound—no footsteps, not the door opening or closing—nothing. As she wiped the tears from her eyes she felt that the girl had simply floated from the room.

To this day, we believe that this was an angel sent from heaven.

As days passed, I continued to cling to life and Mom and my brothers were at last given a glimmer of hope.

"Rhonda has two things going for her," said the doctor, "she's young and if she's a fighter, she may pull through."

For Mom that was money in the bank. At nineteen years of age, not only did I have my youth, but being a body builder,, I was in excellent physical condition. And as for a strong will, no one knew better than my Mother, the brute strength of my will and determination. She knew that I would fight and fight with everything I had and then fight some more!

At last, on December third, I opened my eyes for the first time. They were still unseeing eyes and they quickly closed again. But it was something and Mom was grateful.

That's me at twelve with my little brother, Dom.

Mom was working two jobs at this time to keep her family.

I was eighteen that prom night when I nearly lost my life for the first time.

My older brother, Dean at seventeen was a champion body builder like our dad, though he had no influence on either one of us.

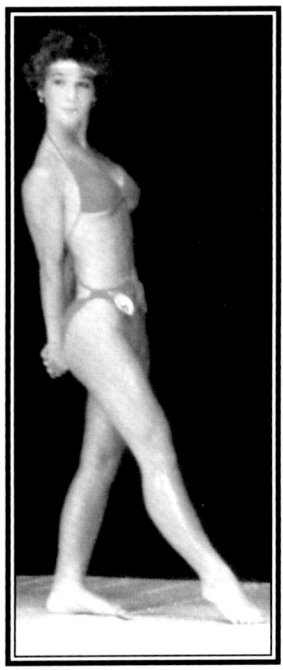

I followed Dean's lead and took up body building.

Since I couldn't attend my own high school graduation, a friend and I took a trip to North Carolina to visit relatives. In the foreground is my cousin Traci Dzurovcin and my friend Julie with me standing.

In June of 1986 Mom and Dom came to visit me in Florida where I was living with my fiancé, Dan.

We enjoyed a day at Disney World during that trip.

Dan, me, Liza and Dean in Florida before Dean and Liza were married, at Bush Gardens

Dean came to visit Dan and me at our home in Lakeland. Dean had no idea at that time what my life was really like.

Mom knew that she had to get me back to Pittsburgh. She had used-up all of her vacation and was forced to go home to work. Now she was traveling back and forth, from Pittsburgh to Florida, every weekend. Not only could she not afford to keep paying the airfare costs, but she desperately needed to figure out a way to be able to pay to have me life-flighted home.

My family and friends back home launched a massive campaign to raise the thousands of dollars that it would take for the life flight. The newspaper wrote about my plight, a bank account was established and before too long, they succeeded in raising an amazing six thousand dollars— enough to pay for a life-flight to bring me home.

While all this effort was being made at home, I managed to show yet another sign of recovery. On December thirteenth, I wept. For a patient in a coma, this is a positive sign—a kind of attempt to swim back up to the surface of consciousness. It was brief but meaningful.

On December 22nd, I was life-flighted to Presbyterian Hospital in Pittsburgh. It was a great relief for Mom to have me home again. At last my Mother and brother and all of the rest of my family could be at my side without having to travel. But soon after my arrival in Pittsburgh, on Christmas day, Dr. John Moossy, the neuro-surgeon assigned to my case, telephoned Mom requesting permission to operate to to save me from certain death. He explained that I had developed hydro-cephalous (water on the brain). He told Mom that my head would have to be shaved and a hole would be drilled into my skull. Dr. Moossy said he would insert a long, thin tube called a V.P. shunt that would, hopefully, drain all of the gathering fluid from the brain.

Mom, of course, agreed to the surgery and Dean made the long drive to be at my bedside in Pittsburgh. On December twenty-ninth, Mom and my brothers waited and prayed. Their prayers were answered. The surgery was successful and soon I was showing even more signs of possibly regaining consciousness. Just two days after surgery, December twenty-seventh, Dom was talking to me, telling me how much I was missed. Curious to see if I could hear him, he asked me if I would hitchhike for him (make the thumb-out sign). My family was elated when, without hesitation, I held up my thumb as though I was trying to hitch a ride. It was my first response in over a month.

I was very fortunate to have done so well with this surgery. Often a patient's body rejects the shunt and the surgery has to be repeated.

But my future was still very much in question. No one could predict if I would ever fully awaken or how much function I would have if I did. It may be none at all or minimal. It was all in God's hands.

On January 7, 1987, I was stable enough to be transferred from Presbyterian Hospital to the nearby Harmarville Rehabilitation Center and placed in the head trauma unit. This brought me even closer to Springdale and our house. I once saw a photograph of myself being taken from the ambulance as I arrived at Harmarville Rehabilitation Center. It was a very cold, wintery day. Mom had put a pretty beige tossel hat that was lined with white fur on my head. Much later, when I looked at that picture of myself, I would notice that I looked just like I was sleeping.

Mom and Dom came faithfully to see me at Harmarville. Every day, there they were, waiting, praying and watching.

In addition, I was now occasionally actually opening my eyes. Though I still wasn't focusing, it was noted on my medical chart that my eyes were darting back and forth—a good sign. But, at this point, still far from conscious and doctors were making no promises.

Meanwhile, the medical training that my older brother, Dean had received in the Air Force enabled him to advise Mom on matters that meant a great deal to my recovery later on. While doctors were still warning that I may spend the rest of my life as little more than a vegetable, Dean was urging Mom to take steps to make sure my body would be ready for therapy once I was out of the coma. One of his suggestions was that the hospital immediately put braces on my legs. Dean warned Mom that since I couldn't move, my legs would begin to bow like a monkeys. Thanks to Dean and Mom's quick action and insistence, I had a head start on my recovery.

But the doctors were still cautious with Mom. They kept telling her that even if I regained consciousness, I may never know anyone or even know who I was. They warned that I may not remember how to walk, talk, or swallow.

But Mom and Dom kept their vigil and were grateful for every sign—agitation, restlessness. Then in early February, on one incredible day, I suddenly began kicking, and flailing with both arms and legs, as if I was fighting my way out of a bag. There I was kicking with those legs that had been still for so long. At last, after moments that seemed like hours of struggling, there came an unnerving almost animal-like sound from somewhere deep inside me—a sound that finally brought me to the surface, awake with eyes wide open, seeing, and focused.

405'S COMING ALIVE!

On a snowy day in February of 1987, a nurse named Fran came running out of a room in the head trauma section of Harmarville Rehabilitation Center. A woman and a teenage boy were leaning over the young girl in the bed—watching, waiting, just as they had been doing for months.

"Four oh five's coming alive!" the nurse yelled while the girl in the bed looked around and wondered where she was.

On that snowy February day I learned that I had lost a piece of my life. Later, I would realize that that was only the beginning of my losses. I awoke on that day not knowing where I was or what day it was. As I looked around, I saw that there were metal bars on both sides of my bed. I had had a dream about bars around my bed. Was it just a dream? The room was very bright and there were three other girls laying in barred beds. They all appeared to be sleeping.

As I swam up to full consciousness, I was relieved to see my Mother and younger brother standing to the left of my bed. Relief and then confusion. They lived in Pittsburgh. I lived in Lakeland, Florida. What were they doing in Florida?

Where are we? How did you get here? What is happening? I tried to ask all of this but nothing would come out of my mouth. I didn't feel sick. I didn't even have a headache. I was in no pain. I was just terribly confused.

I hadn't realized it then but God was with me through it all. My mom said that I could have been crippled, maimed, or burnt. But I wasn't any of the above, thank God!

I noticed large windows to one side of the room and I saw

AWAKE

that it was snowing. *Snowing? Snowing! It doesn't snow in Florida. Where am I?*

Seeing the look of panic on my face as I tried desperately to speak, my mother began to explain to me that I had been in a terrible accident almost three months earlier! They hadn't seen any response since December twenty-seventh when I hitch-hiked for Dom. Mom was, of course, elated to see me awake even though she was still in shock over my leaving home just after I turned eighteen. Now, only a year and a half later, I was fighting for my life.

Three months? Three months! I've been sleeping for three months!

She told me that I had survived a great trauma. She said that on a Tuesday evening back in November, *November?*, at approximately seven-thirty I was returning home from my job at the dance studio. I had just taken a co-worker named Shelly home. *Dance studio? Shelly?* None of this meant anything to me. It was like hearing a story about someone else.

What I didn't understand until later was that I had lost more than my memory of time. I had lost my memory of functions like breathing, swallowing, talking, walking. It was all gone! *Unbelievable! Please, somebody, please pinch me.*

My Mother went on to tell me that the car crash occurred as I was heading toward the trailer where I lived. When I realized that I had missed my usual turn, I attempted to make a u-turn to correct this and was hit broadside by a drunk driver. My car, she said, was demolished.

I was stunned, unable to grasp what she was saying. It was all so confusing. As my mother continued to repeat my situation to me, and I slowly I began to comprehend. I did remember that I lived in Florida and that my family lived in Pennsylvania. But I didn't remember working in a dance studio or knowing someone named Shelly. It was as if all of the things that were close in time to the accident, had vanished from my memory. I would soon learn that this was a common occurrence, as it is the brain's way of protecting the body.

As gently as possible, my Mother continued to explain that I had been rushed to Lakeland Regional Medical Center. She said I was in the Lakeland Hospital, clinging to life, for two weeks. Then, once I stabilized a little, I was life-flighted back to Pittsburgh's Presbyterian Hospital. There I had emergency life-saving surgery to relieve the pressure on my brain caused by a build-up of fluid. The neuro-surgeon, Dr. John Moossy, saved my life and now, my Mother told me, I was at the Harmarville Rehabilitation Center, not far from home.

A drunk driver? What was his condition? So, I'm home in Pittsburgh. How could this be possible?

As difficult and horrible as all of this was to accept, the most disturbing moments came when her story referred to my life before the accident—a life I could not recall.

She told me that my boyfriend had taken off after the accident.

My boyfriend? I have a boyfriend?

My Mother said that he, Dan, she said his name was, had taken our belongings from the trailer we shared and left without a word. She felt terrible telling me this but I had no idea what or who she was talking about and I felt nothing but confusion. Mom went on to tell me that my friends told her how Dan, who had a drinking problem, had severely beaten me just two days before the accident. But that brutal beating mercifully, had vanished in the car crash along with many other things. I've been told that it's better that I didn't remember, otherwise I might have nightmares for the rest of my life.

A coma is a strange thing. While my memories of everything that happened just before the accident were gone, I do have some bits of memory of being in the coma. I remember always being cold and hungry. I remember thinking that I had died and believing that I must have been judged to be a very bad person to have ended up like this.

I also remember what must have been dreams. One was unremarkable where I was watching television in the living room of my Mother's house with my two brothers. After sitting with them for awhile, I got up and went to bed. Another dream was disturbing.

My Mother and my boyfriend, Dan's mother. (though I couldn't consciously remember Dan, I was able to dream about him and as time passed I understood that the other woman in the dream was Dan's Mother.) were shopping together. In this dream they were looking at beautiful clothes. Dan's Mom held up a dress and said, "It's too bad Rhonda has to be gone, she would love this dress."

Then my Mother held up another dress and said, "Rhonda would look gorgeous in this one too." Then she started to cry.

It seemed that I was floating somewhere above them and when I heard them say these things, I began to wave my arms and shout, *"I'm not dead! I'm here!"* But they never saw me or heard me and they just walked out of the store.

In another dream I was laying still in a bed with bars all around it. A very thin and pale man was circling my bed and I remember thinking, *"Oh God, I've been really bad. I died and have been sent to hell and this is the devil."*

I was later told that a doctor had walked around my bed and of course, since I was in a coma, my bed of course, did have bars for protection.

In the early days, as I was just regaining consciousness, I have vague memories of my Mother and sometimes a nurse helping me to shower. And even though I wasn't fully conscious, I remember knowing for certain that I hated being cared-for like a baby—wearing a diaper, being fed, having my teeth brushed for me. I would even weep with humiliation when my Mom cared for me, *"My God why can't I even brush my own teeth!"*

Once I was more alert, I insisted on choosing what clothes I would wear each day. Every morning, my recreation therapist, Lori, would come into my room and take some clothes from the closet. I would point to what I wanted to wear.

On Valentines Day, not long after I awakened, my Mother got me all dressed, put a brown wig on my head to cover the area that had been shaved for surgery back at the hospital, and put me in a wheelchair for a grand tour of what was to be my home for the next four months. Though I hated the wheelchair, it was an amazing experience to be taken into the bustling hallway of the rehab center, past a gift shop and into a lounge where the television was on.

Since I couldn't talk, I was given a Canon Communicator so that I would be able to speak by typing what I had to say. But before long, I devised my own sign language even though I only had the use of my left arm. Though my right arm was not paralyzed, it was weak and shook uncontrollably. My doctors, Dr. Greim and Dr. Mosley hadn't wasted any time getting me started on a regular physical therapy routine. Soon my days were filled with five therapies five days a week.

My speech would eventually come back, but for a long time I wasn't able to make an 's' sound. So when my Mother would call and ask what I was doing, I would say I was 'leaping' instead of sleeping. When I was alone, I would lay in my bed and practice making different sounds involving the letters s and ch.

I would stress to anyone going through this—never give up on yourself and most of all, don't give up on prayer and God.

One day Mom wheeled me into the gift shop. Immediately I spotted a cute teddy bear that was dressed in military fatigues. This to me was a reminder of my big brother, Dean, who is in the Air Force. I began pointing to it with my left hand (since my right hand was disabled by seizures) and gesturing that I wanted it. I was getting pretty good at sign language and Mom was getting pretty good at understanding. She bought me the bear (which I still cherish to this day) along with my angel pin and a big stuffed dog.

This goes back to when I was still in the coma and Mom and Dom were trying to stimulate me with talk and music. They had been told that a patient's hearing is believed to be the last to go no matter how deep the coma. They made a tape recording for me with Dean and Dom urging me to wake up and telling me how much they missed me. They even had my beloved dog, Daisy Mae barking and, in her own way, begging me to wake-up. That tape is something I still treasure. And I told Mom that if she had been able to bring Daisy Mae to me, I guarantee that if I had felt her hot, puppy breath on my face, I would have awakened a lot faster. I love dogs and I believe that they have tremendous healing powers because they are so full of love and dedication.

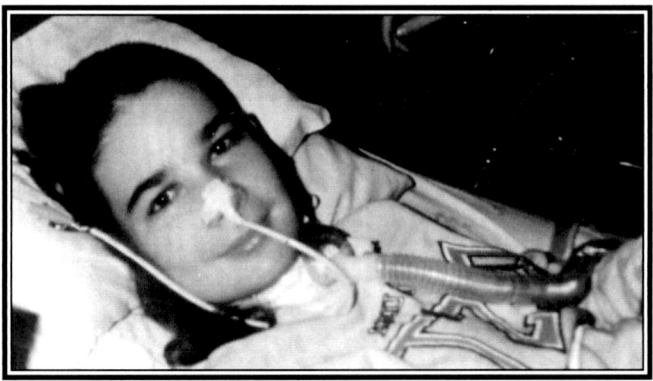

This was the day I woke up after three months in a coma.

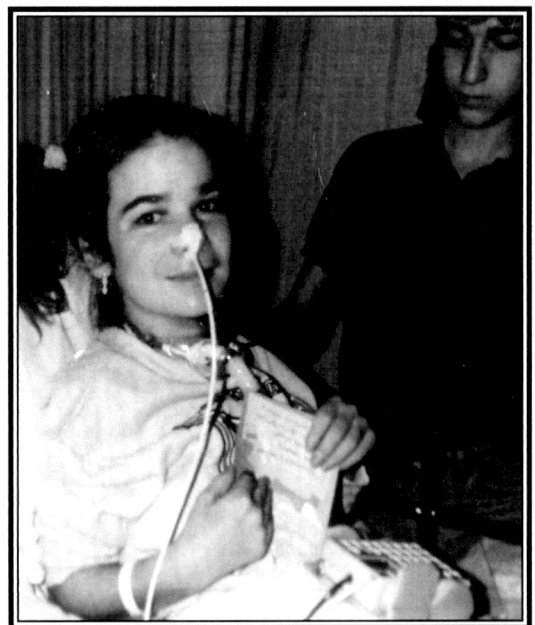

That's Dom with me shortly after I woke up. Dom and Mom were with me every step of the way. That's the Cannon Communicator on my lap. I had to use that until I could speak again. You can see that my right arm is weak and curled inward and, of course, I still have a nasogastric tube as well as the trachea tube that aided my breathing. As for my youthful appearance, it is not unusual for someone newly-awake from a coma to appear much younger than their actual age.

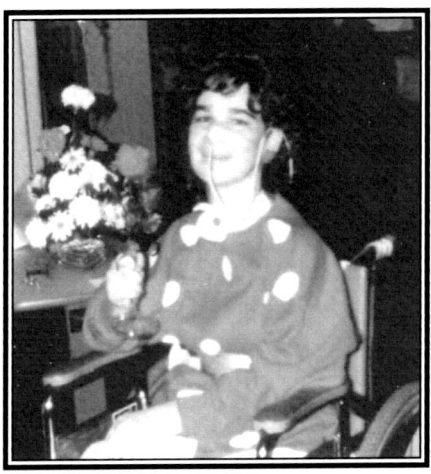

Mom made sure I was all dressed-up for Valentines Day, complete with a curly wig to cover the area where they had shaved my head for surgery.

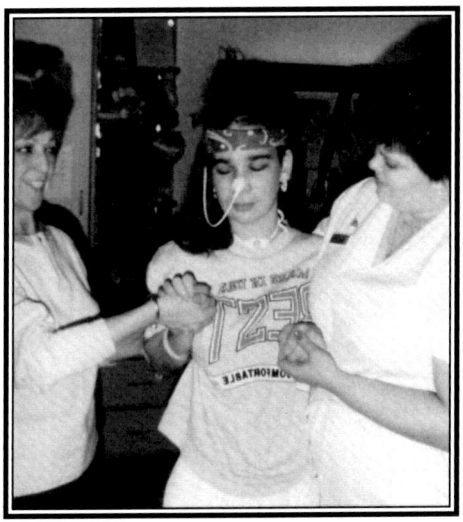

Mom and Roberta, one of my wonderful Harmarville nurses, help me to walk. Mom always had my earings, watch, and sometimes a headband to match my outfit. This is my personality, always matching.

AWAKE

It would take me a long time before I learned that sometimes God allows you to experience terrible times for very good reasons and that through it all, He loves you unconditionally. I was to learn that God never lets you be hurt unnecessarily and that eventually everything makes sense. We know that *God causes all things to work together for good, to those who love God, to those who are called according to His purpose. - Romans 8:28*

As time went on, my Mother told me more about my being in a coma. She described how my body had curled into a fetal position and told me that the doctors told her to expect the worst. She said that they told her to go home to Pittsburgh to begin making funeral arrangements for me. I can only imagine what a horror it was for her as a single parent, to be told that her only daughter, her nineteen year old daughter, was going to die.

I'm so grateful to God for seeing her through all of this. I don't think I could have done it if I had been the mother. But then "God's grace is sufficient for everything." Although I didn't realize this fully at the time. I kept thinking that if, as they say, God never gives you more than you can handle—what about this! Surely, he can see the torment I'm living with?

I never got a verbal answer from Him but over time he gave me an understanding and the sure knowledge that His word is true. *He will never leave or forsake you.* But at the time, I was so lonely and empty-feeling, I didn't realize that he was with me the whole way.

During this period I felt nothing but hatred for the drunk driver who hit me. I was in a terrible self-pity trap and I saw no way out. My despair gave me great emotional pain—my head felt numb and all of my insides felt like they were slowly being ripped out.

I know now that it took all of this pain for me to have a spiritual awakening though it might have been easier if I had been taught, as a child, about God and faith. But that's not the way it was.

When I awoke with so many unwanted changes, I felt empty and desperate I had lost my memory, my strength, my freedom, my voice, my job, my fiancé, my car. But, much later, in my desperation, I turned to Him. I begged Him to come into my life and give me peace. I know that I received my faith after I received His peace. And all the while he was working on my character. But I would have to travel a long, lonely and difficult road before I would gain full realization of all of this.

During those winter days just after I came out of my coma, I was in the depths of despair. I really felt that on that November evening I had really lost my life in Florida. It may sound strange but I believed then that my spirit and the true Rhonda was really dead.

I hated my loss of control. I hated the degradation of having to be wheeled into a shower to have someone bath me! I hated having my diaper changed. It was horrible! Every time some one had to take care of my personal needs, I'd cry like a baby from humiliation.

I was always strong willed. I hated relying on someone for everything. I never wanted anyone's sympathy—not Mom's, not the doctors', not anyone's!

The long and lonely road

THERE WERE MANY doctors and nurses involved in my recovery process, but there are four nurses that I will never forget. They were with me back in the coma rooms and they became like family to me. Fran, Donna, Marilyn and Barb are very special people to me. Fran and Donna were like my mothers when Mom couldn't be there. Marilyn kept me laughing and continued her friendship even after I was discharged. Barb, a devout Christian, was beautiful, positive and encouraging. It was Barb who gave me my first Christian cassette, *Mylon and Broken Heart*. She would always say, "Rhonda, I hate to see you cry every day. God loves you so much, he's allowed this to happen for a very special reason and you'll understand His plan for you some day."

Ten years later I contacted her and invited her to come to hear me give my testimony at the Salvation Army. I was honored that she came.

Almost immediately after awakening, I was taken into physical therapy. Mom was there watching and I was so ashamed that I couldn't even hold my head up. I was once a body builder, and now I couldn't control my own head.

Please, God, I was thinking, *let me be able to do something while Mom is watching.* But later Mom told me even though I looked like a rag doll, she was so grateful to see me alive and working hard just to hold my head up because my muscles were still so weak. Shortly after, I was given both a cane and a walker to aide my steps. They were both quickly taken away when the therapists saw that I was only carrying them. *Glory to God, they weren't needed!* Next, we would work on turning my baby steps into normal steps.

In the midst of my pain and suffering, I met Paul. Paul was a recreation therapist. Amazingly, he was a former head-injury patient and he had endured the same things that I was going through. He had been caught in an explosion where he used to work. And now he could walk and talk and think just as he had before the accident. He was only a few years older than me. We liked the same kind of music and we enjoyed talking to each other. Paul knew what I was experiencing and he made me feel comfortable even when my words came out jumbled or mispronounced.

It was because of Paul's encouragement that I poured my emotions into writing a song.

Why Me

Oh, God, I woke up one day and didn't have the slightest idea where I was why me

All I remember are terrible things like a bunch of needles in my arms oh, God, why me

And I remember thinking I was in hell why me

I was always begging God to take me away oh God, why me

Now you can see the sadness in my eyes why me

I want so bad to be back to normal and in Florida oh God, why me

I must be getting punished for something why me

God, don't you understand how sad I am oh God, why me

I want out of this position and can't be why me

I cry every day but it doesn't help me oh God, why me

I wish sometime that I could cry myself to death why me

I hope to God that some day soon, I'll be back to normal oh God, why me

God, don't you know how bad the pain is why me and it never goes away. It only gets worse

Oh god why me why me

Paul sat with me as I wrote my song. He held my hand as I wrote and cried. I was always crying.

In the years before the accident, I had been rebellious. My mother disapproved of my boyfriend, Dan who she knew to be a heavy drinker. But I would not listen to my Mother.

"It's my life and I'll do what I want!" I'd say a million times when she would try to convince me to break-up with Dan.

On the positive side, I followed in my brother's footsteps and developed an interest in body building. I worked hard at the gym before I met Dan. In the long, lonely hours and days at Harmarville Rehab. I would often tell God how much I wished that I could erase the two years before the accident so that this chaos cold have been prevented.

As my birthday approached, Mom began counting down the days on a calendar that was hanging next to my bed. She noticed, however, that the more days she counted off, the more I squinted to see the dates. She notified my doctors immediately and I was soon wearing glasses.

MARCH 10, 1987

Today is my twentieth birthday. I'm very excited and not just because of all the gifts I'll be getting but because of something Mom just told me. She said that my older brother, Dean is coming to see me today! He's in the Air Force in Pensacola, Florida and Mom said he's anxious to see me now that I'm awake. The last time he saw me I was unconscious and in Presbyterian Hospital in Pittsburgh.

I was thrilled. She said he would be staying for two weeks and would come to all of my classes with me. But then she shocked me by telling me that Dean would be bringing his wife and daughter! I have no memory of a wife and daughter. *Later, I would come to understand that he married someone of great patience and understanding. They had only been married months before my accident and she had to endure much time without her new husband as he drove back to*

AWAKE

Pennsylvania to be by my side.

Since I still can't talk, I'll type Dean a message telling him how great it is to see him!

It's bedtime now. I celebrated my birthday as best as I could in the hospital. Having Dean drive all the way from Florida was the best part! And the way he surprised me when he arrived was great!

I was out in the hall, sitting in my wheelchair not expecting him until later when I suddenly heard this voice behind my ear.

"Would you like a ride somewhere, little girl?"

I can't explain the joy in my heart to hear his voice. I thought, *is it really Dean?* I turned around and he gave me a big kiss and a hug. I'm surprised the excitement didn't kill me.

Dean became like a father to me since our real dad never acknowledged us. All of this brings back a memory: When I first awakened from my coma so confused, I would tell myself that if all of this was really true then surely my dad would be here with me. But he never came. Never.

I don't know why that surprises me. On my seventeenth birthday I asked my Mother why I never received a birthday card from my dad. Though she had no answer for me, she suggested that I might phone him. At first I didn't want to but then I decided that I should. Mom had to dial the number because I didn't even know it. I was nervous when I heard his voice but I managed to say, "this is your daughter, Rhonda. It's my birthday today."

"Excuse me," he said.

So I repeated. "This is Rhonda, your daughter. It's my birthday today."

Quickly he answered, "I'm sorry, you have the wrong number." And he simply hung up.

It is amazing that I survived the accident at all. I had lost so much blood that I was given a blood transfusion at the accident scene. And because I was lying still so long in a coma, I suffered two bouts of pneumonia and was only given a three to five percent chance of surviving. And, even if I survived, doctors told my family that I might remain comatose for the rest of my life, since I had already started reverting to the fetal position. I've been a pretty blessed girl, wouldn't you say?

When I think about all of this, I think about the poem, "Footprints." Just as the poem says, I know that during this time of helplessness, God was carrying me. He has taken me from death's door more than a few times.

One of the reasons that I couldn't talk was that I had had a breathing tube in my throat. I hated it when the nurses had to clean and suction that horrible hole in my throat. It was gross and painful and I would shake uncontrollably during the whole procedure. On the day after my twentieth birthday, the trachea was removed! Dean was there and he held my hand while the doctor worked to take it out.

Over that winter and early spring as I continued my rehabilitation at Harmarville Rehabilitation Center, I began to remember more and more of my past. I kept writing in my journal as my depression deepened.

I was thrilled to have Dean and his family home with me for my birthday. Pictured here are my Uncle Larry, me, Dom in the background, Dean, and Larry's daughter, Melissa.

While Dean was home on that visit, he attended my therapies with me and was wonderfully supportive.

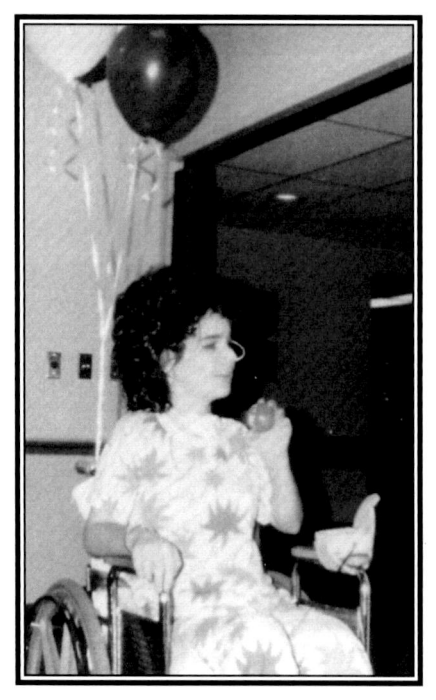

Dean gave me a red ball to work with to help strengthen my hand. (I have my wig on in this picture.)

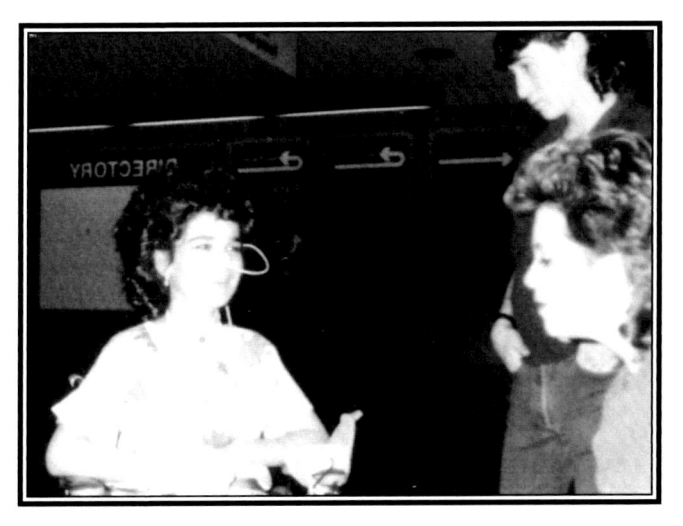

I always enjoyed visits from family and friends. Here I am with Becky and Dom.

My birthday was over, Dean and his family had gone back to Florida, and I was terribly confused when I had this phone conversation with Dean.

AWAKE

APRIL 6, 1987

I went to sleep last night after crying for about an hour. The same thing happened to me today after my last class. I thought about living in Florida with Dan and the fun times we had. Too bad, there were just as many bad times. When Dan and I first arrived in Florida we drove right into hurricane Elena. That was pretty scary but I had no idea how much more frightening life would get with Dan.

I remember the early days in Florida when we were living in Tarpon Springs. Dan was working construction and we were living in a motel. I would be alone all day and he would come home, eat, take a shower and go out to the bars for several hours, leaving me alone again.

I was so sad and angry that he would leave me to sit alone in a strange place. We lived very near Lake Hollingsworth and I spent many lonely hours looking at the beauty all around us. One evening I got so furious that I actually walked to a few of the bars looking for Dan. But I never did it again because it was too dark and scary.

I don't understand all of these changes and I *hate* them so bad! I wish I could turn the clock back about three years.

APRIL 7, 1987

Today was boring, as usual. I'm still quite depressed. I wish this never, ever happened. It seems like I'm either watching some horror movie or having a really bad dream. 'everyone here runs my life now. Sometimes I think I'd be better off dead.

APRIL 8, 1987

I still have two really good friends that come to see me occasionally—Becky and Carolyn. Carolyn and I have been close friends since elementary school. Becky and I met when we were both sophomores in high school. Mom is happy to have them visit me because neither of them like Dan. Carolyn and I used to go to an under twenty-one dance nightclub and dance'till we dropped. We loved it so much. Becky never went with us. She grew up working with her dad on big trucks so she is pretty much a tomboy. We met because I asked her if she was interested in buying two brand new pairs of pumps that I had. She bought both pairs and we have been friends ever since.

I wonder if I'll ever dance again.

April 9, 1987

Today is a new day and I can already tell that it's going to be another bad day. I already feel really down. I haven't even done anything yet. Why does my life have to be like this now?

April 10, 1987

Last night NOBODY came in to see me—not even Mom! I hate this place so bad. It's so lonely here. I could die.

I cannot believe how very much my Mom and brothers hate Dan. They don't ever want him near me again. I wonder if I'll ever understand where all of their hate is coming from. I know I make them very sad every time I mention his name. No one has any idea what I'm going through. I swear the confusion will make my poor head explode and I believe the anguish is going to make my heart stop beating. Maybe I am already dead and these are just a bunch of demons playing games with my mind and heart. *"Oh, please God, take me out of here now!"*

April 11, 1987

Mom just called and made me really happy talking to me about my puppy at home. Her name is Daisy Mae. She started out being my little brother's pet, but I claimed ownership when he became too old to have a puppy. He got her from Becky's farm a couple of years ago.

April 12, 1987

Today I'm going to tell Mom again that I'm going to try really hard not to mention Dan anymore. I don't ever want her or my brothers to be mad at me. I love them too much. I hope that some day soon, I'll remember clearly the facts they are telling me about Dan. Though I do have memories of other beatings from him, I cannot remember that last and most brutal one. I wish I could remember so that it would be easier to forget him.

April 13, 1987

Today was boring, as usual! I don't think that there is ever a day that I'm not sad and bored. I got some really pretty flowers from Dan's family for Easter and a post card from Dean. I really like to wheel myself into the television room to watch *Moonlighting* because Bruce Willis reminds me of Dean.

I saved a lot of my notes from my stay at Harmarville Rehab. One page that I kept is a copy of a tic-tac-toe game I played with Mom. On that same paper she wrote down some names from my life in Florida. She wrote down the name of the dance studio where I worked. It was called Cabaret. And I immediately knew that she was right. I remembered that name. Then she wrote the names of my Boss, Diane and a co-worker, Shelly. But these meant nothing to me. I couldn't even picture their faces. Later, while I was thinking about it, I suddenly knew exactly who Diane was. But I couldn't remember Shelly at all. That seemed strange to me since Shelly was the last person I saw before I had the accident.

I had been told that Shelly and I had left work together and I had just driven her home.

As time went by, I began remembering picking Shelly up that morning and being at work all day. I also remembered that I was having trouble with my car stalling. When I went to Shelly's house that morning, her dad looked at my car and told me it was the solenoid. He said to bring it back after work and he would fix it. But I don't remember anything about taking her home. I've tried to concentrate in order to get back some vision or memory, but no luck.

I have been told that it is possible that my car stalled when I made that u-turn. It is possible that the driver who hit me, drunk as he was, assumed I would have been out of the way by the time he got to where my car was. When I saw the photos of the accident site. The road was flat and straight. The land on either side of the road was flat. There were no ditches or guard rails. There was nothing but empty field on either side of that road. A driver, even a driver who was speeding, could have swerved to avoid hitting me and never even damage his car. But that driver would have had to be sober and have his wits about him. The one who hit me did not.

Each time Mom and Dom would come to see me they would try to do something to keep me alert and thinking. They would get me to play catch with a pair of socks rolled up in a ball. Being that my right side was paralyzed, I didn't do well but I would try anyway. They would also check my cognitive skills by saying a word and having me type the correct spelling. I always loved to spell and I did well with this. They would give me math problems and have me type the correct answer. Mom would ask me the color of her blouse or earrings and I would nod when she said the correct color.

I was lucky to be able to play a game like tic-tac-toe. My printing, however, was very large and sloppy, like a childs. Everything I did took a lot of thought and practice. It was like starting over as an infant and it was harder than hard.

April 14, 1987

As soon as I was out of the coma, I had an overwhelming urge to tell mom every intimate secret. God only knows why I felt that I had to do this. But there I was, not even able to speak, typing every last detail on my Canon Communicator.

(Actually, I had a need to repent and since I had not known Jesus as my savior yet, Mom was the closest in my life.)

I told Mom that during my senior year of high school I got mixed-up with a couple of really wild guys and that we had been doing drugs. I must have been temporarily insane. Then I told her about one of her male friends who come on to me when I was only sixteen. I explained that he had come by one day while she was working. He took me for a motorcycle ride and asked me to put my hand where it definitely should not have been! I completely ignored him, acted like I couldn't hear him over the motorcycle and we just rode back home. At the time, I kept trying to make myself believe that he really didn't do that because I couldn't believe that he was really a pervert and he was.

I described for my Mom how I had gotten deliriously drunk on prom night because I had planned to meet-up with Dan at midnight and leave my prom date behind.

But while the accident made me want to confess everything to my Mother, I still didn't have the grace to stop making stupid choices.

My neuropsychology therapist, Suzie has started a log book for me to help me remember what I do each day and why. I will be giving it to each therapist so that they can write a note for me.

April 15, 1987

Therapist's notes: Psychology (Manny)

Rhonda was in a much better, brighter mood than she was last week. Over the weekend she came to the conclusion that she did not want to fight with her mother and brother and get them mad at her. That was a good insight....and hopefully now Rhonda will be able to get back on the right track in therapy.

(Not so quick with that assumption!)

April 16, 1987

Tonight I wheeled myself down to the gym. The reason I went was because I wanted to see this really cute therapist named Gino. I found Gino lifting weights in the gym. I hope that some day I can life weights again.

When I got back to my room, Mom called and said she was upset with me because I had told her about an old high school friend who had called me. The friend is Dan's cousin. Roxanne. Mom now hates anyone who has any connection to Dan.

My roommate, Joan, left today. She gave me some pretty flowers and a card. We had always laughed and told each other that some day we'd each write a book about our experiences.

April 17, 1987

Therapist's notes: Psychology (Manny)
We discussed the inappropriateness of constant giggling and the reasons why it is potentially dangerous for Rhonda to have contact with Dan, Roxanne and others related to him. We discussed Rhonda's lack of insight, judgement, and maturity at the present time.

Today was really awful. It all started after lunch. They couldn't hear my naso-gastric (NG) tube so they gave me a new one. But that one fell out so they had to give me another. I was so enraged that I had to be held down so they could shove the tubes up my nose and down my throat. It felt so very awful. I was squirming, screaming and crying. I even tried to hold my nose so that couldn't stick anything in it. But there were just too many hands holding me down.

After they got my NG tube back in, I started thinking about how I first found out about my shunt. It was shortly after I awoke from the coma. I was very curious about everything. Since I was unable to speak, I couldn't ask anyone so I just started feeling all over my body to see what was wrong with me. (I only had the use of my left arm at this time since my right arm shook uncontrollably.) I started with my feet. They seemed fine so I tried my legs. Just above my left knee there seemed to be a large burn. Next I found a scar just above and to the right of my belly button. There was one tiny scar on the first joint of my right hand which I later found out was caused by flying glass from my windshield.

When I touched my neck and face everything felt normal. It's strange that before the accident, I would look at myself in the mirror and see a short, plain girl looking back at me. But during that long, three-month sleep, God seemed to give a new pair of eyes. All through high school I idolized every glamour model I ever saw and wanted that life and as a result, I wanted desperately to be tall and built like a poker. After I awoke, I was really pleased with my appearance. I was grateful for my looks and not in a conceited way, just very grateful for the way God made me. And to this day, I couldn't be happier with what I see looking back at me.

But on my first day out of the coma, I did find a little bump on the back, right side of my head. This was something new and very peculiar to me. It wasn't big but it really troubled me. That night when my Mom came back to see me, I took her hand and placed it on the bump on my head and shrugged. She understood why I was curious.

She looked so worried and serious as she sat down. *What's the big deal? I was just in a car wreck and got my head banged around.*

Mom told me I had been in a very serious accident, more serious than I had realized. She told me that I was nearly killed. That everyone thought I would surely die from all the trauma. When the doctors realized that fluid was building up on my brain, they had told her that the only way to save my life was to operate and insert a permanent VP (ventriculoperitoneal) shunt to drain the fluid from my brain into my bladder. It was placed between a cerebral ventricle and the abdomen.

My Mother told me that she was afraid to tell me all of this because she thought I would flip out. But she was surprised at how well I handled it.

Actually, I seemed to handle it well because I couldn't yet comprehend it. Later I would be able to joke about it and call myself the bionic woman.

April 19, 1987

Today I went home for Easter. I had so much fun. I didn't ever want to come back. It was neat. I walked around the whole house all by myself. Imagine, a twenty-year old getting so excited about walking alone! Mom and Dean helped me but at first it was really terrifying. I was so afraid of falling and hitting my head. I was afraid of the hard, shiny floors. Just the sight of them would make me cry. But that was part of my new life with that skinny, tube in my head. I used to walk briskly or run without thinking about anything.

April 21, 1987

Therapist's notes: Neurobehavior (Suzie)

We reviewed log book and Suzie felt that you hadn't been putting enough effort into getting it filled out. We talked about not using your problems as an excuse for not working at your therapy. We talked about having you try to ask other people how they are—to make more effort to respond to them.

I was really depressed today because my neurobehavior instructor told me that I have no manners. (I didn't realize it at the time, but she was just watching for my reaction and my reaction was bad. Instead of accepting it as constructive criticism, I cried and yelled again.) I was so furious about it. I was cheered a little though when my Mother came this evening.

April 22, 1987

I had a fairly good day today, although I'm glad it's over with. I started thinking about how cold I was when I was in the coma. I know that sometimes I was cold because I had wet myself. I had a problem with that for a long time after I awoke, for a few years in fact.

April 23, 1987

Therapist's notes: (Suzie)
Rhonda greeted me with " How are you," which was a first and made her feel great!

April 24, 1987

Therapist's notes: Neurobehavior (Suzie)
Worked more on family tree and again it got a lot easier with some practice. Rhonda's doing a great job remembering to talk to people a little more. It really helps.

April 25, 1987

Today was really good and Mom just left. Now you should take note of that. I don't say I had too many good days.

April 26, 1987

Dear God, I just cried a million tears. I wish so bad that you would take me out of this situation and this place! I don't understand why Dan beat me or why I had to be in this terrible accident. *Why?*

Today the nurses informed Mom that I am not allowed off the unit any more. The only good thing about this day is that both Mom and Dom came to see me.

April 27, 1987

I just got a letter from Dean and it was so nice to get. But these nurses really make me so mad. I was bored and had nothing to do so I got a cigarette from another patient and smoked it. That is, until they saw me and took it away from me telling me that I am not allowed to smoke.

I wish they weren't always running my life. I feel like I'm in prison here. I lay awake at night and think that this would be the perfect punishment for a criminal. You have every privilege and every right stripped from you. You have no control of anything. This is like total blackness, emptiness and despair, just like Alcatraz, only this is Harmarville!! *(I was obviously not in a good state of mind. Now, many years later, I am very grateful for Harmarville because they helped me a lot.)*

As soon as I could wheel myself around Harmarville, I located some pay phones and soon I was always on the phone to Mom, my friend Kara, my brother, and even eventually, Dan. Amazingly, I remembered Dan's parents' phone number. When I phoned there his mother told me how happy she was to hear from me. She told me how much Dan missed me and she also said she would let him know where I was so that he could start calling me—and he did. The very next day he called me and he continued to call me every day after that.

Needless to say, mom and my brothers wold be furious if they had any idea that I was communicating with Dan again.

April 28, 1987

Surprisingly today was a good day. I took a nap right after dinner and Uncle Eddie, Uncle Larry, and Aunt Eileen were all there when I woke up. What a nice surprise. I love visitors.

When it's over, though, I always think about how lucky they are to be able to walk out to their cars and drive themselves home and do whatever they want without asking permission. People have no idea how much they take for granted every day. I think of times when I was so happy like when Dean and his future wife drove from Pensacola to visit Dan and me in Lakeland. The four of us spent a day at Busch Gardens and it was really fun. Then, another time, Mom and Dom came down from Pennsylvania. We all spent a day at Disney World. Sadly, they were both stressful days for me because I knew Dan would get back to drinking as soon as my family was gone.

Mom came in shortly after my other visitors. She had something important to show me. She had documented letters from two close friends of mine in Florida. In the letters they were testifying about the last beating I received from Dan.

One letter described how Dan and I were inside our trailer and how he was beating me on the Sunday before my accident.

I didn't know what to make of this since I still couldn't remember that last beating.

Our neighbor, P.J. wrote "He was beating her so bad that their trailer was bouncing from one end to the other."

One letter also said that Dan was now dating another friend of mine. What a creep!

Mom also told me that I'll be going home in a month or two. I thought that sounded great. I cannot wait for that day!

Aunt Eileen just cut my hair short. I guess it looks alright.

May 2, 1987

Today I went home for a short visit. It sure was nice to be back home. This rehab is now my second home—how depressing! When I was out in the hall, I met a man named Matt. He was here visiting him mother. He's really, really handsome. He kissed me on the cheek!

Awake

May 8, 1987

They finally took my NG tube out. Now I'm eating real food! This morning Kara called. She's a really nice girl that I met out in the hall one day. She told me that she was once a patient here. She calls and visits me often. I know that she must remember how lonely and boring this place can be.

I just ate dinner and unfortunately Thelma sat next to me. She talked ninety miles an hour. I am not exaggerating!

What I want more than anything is to talk the way I used to. I'm not worried about walking again because I think it's coming if I could just get over this fear of falling.

I went to speech therapy every day for four months. My words were unclear, I had no volume and my voice was very nasal. It was terrifying to me that I was unable to make certain sounds. My speech teacher used to tape me relearning to speak. When he would play the tapes back, I would just sob. It would be years before I could speak normally.

Mom and my brother had hired an attorney in Florida to represent me. My lawyer said that the man who hit me was just a bum and didn't have anything worth taking. He said that the car didn't even belong to the driver, but to his girl friend. And he said, all of the criminal charges against him were dropped on a legal technicality because the paramedic who took the blood levels wasn't certified. So much for justice!

The Florida Highway Patrol established that the wreck was sixty-five percent the fault of the drunk driver and thirty-five percent my fault for making the u-turn. They established that it took his car one hundred twenty feet to come to a stop and my car eighty feet.

When the driver learned that my family was attempting to sue him, he filed suit against my Mother since she was my legal guardian. He sued for one hundred thousand dollars because he received one hundred stitches on his cheek from the accident.

In the end, my insurance company actually paid this man eight thousand dollars to settle out of court!

So here is this drunk who shouldn't have been driving in the first place, smashing into my car, leaving me in a coma and walking away from it all with eight thousand dollars!

He probably has no idea what he did to my life. He almost killed me and now most of the time I wish I was dead. Besides being in a coma, sustaining severe head injuries and being left partially brain-damaged, there is so much emotional damage now too.

That was me then. But seeing it now, I know that if I hadn't had the accident, I would never have gotten myself out of the terrible lifestyle I was in. I was too ashamed to ever tell anyone how Dan was treating me so I just put up with it. So the nurse Barb was absolutely right. God allowed this awful wreck to happen for a very good reason.

May 12, 1987

Today I cried my eyes out in Vocational. I am so sick of crying so much and always being sad and confused. I wish I could just die now so that I wouldn't have to feel all of this confusion. I wish I could have a normal life.

When I was home for my visit, I had Mom take me for a ride past my Dad's house. I don't' even feel right calling him my Dad. He's just Ron to me. Anyway, he was outside and we stopped and talked to him for a few minutes. He told me that now that he knows that I am at Harmarville Rehab., he'll call me to see how I'm coming along.

I won't hold my breath, he really sickens me. He's so cold. I don't know how he sleeps at night. How can a man create two lives and never acknowledge them?

Everyone says that he'll pay severely on judgement day but I want him to pay NOW!

The doctor was just in and he said that I've come a long way. But I don't see the changes. I can't wait until I can look back on this as a bad memory. I hope I will be back to normal in the near future.

May 17, 1987

Today was pretty good. Mom was here again of course.

Awake

Yesterday was really bad because I finally told Mom that Dan's mother came to see me. Mom was really, really mad. I cried a couple of rivers.

This photo of my cars illustrates the intensity of the impact that was a direct hit on the driver's side.

When you study this photograph of the accident scene, complete with skid marks, it's clear that a sober driver could have easily avoided hitting me by swerving onto the wide open and level roadside.

May 19, 1987

Mom and Dom were here today. Aunt Eileen cut my hair again. I've never had my hair this short before. It's always been long and permed. Last night Dan called and I told him never to call me again and to tell his Mother not to visit me any more. He sounded really disgusted. He said that he would never forget me and he promised that some day he would come for me and I believe he will. It wasn't easy saying what I said to him but I knew that I had to.

May 20, 1987

I just got back from attending a Pittsburgh Pirate game with some other patients. It was nice to get out of here but I was cold and bored and, of course, I ended up balling my eyes out. I started to feel sad on the bus. I was remembering some things with Dan. I feel like I'm missing a big part of my life. It's like I'm a robot or a freak now. I never get to make any decisions myself and I hate that.

Why has this happened to me?

May 27, 1987

Today we had a speaker for group. His name was Jamie Russo. He was very encouraging because years ago, he too suffered a head injury. You would never have known that anything ever happened to him. I hope I get to that point someday.

I am constantly thinking about the way I used to be—the way I used to walk, talk, laugh. I just end up depressing myself. I wonder if God will let me get everything back.

I will restore unto you the years that the locusts have eaten.
- Joel 2:25

He has, He has and I thank Him every day!

May 30, 1987

Today I got to go boating with Mom and Aunt Carol. I thought about Dan the whole time, wishing he was there. Maybe the memories of him will diminish in time but it will be a long, long, time.

Even though I had tried to listen to Mom and cut all ties with Dan, we had been secretly talking on the phone every day. Dan was always telling me how much he missed me and how lonely he was without me. He told me that he just had to drive from Florida to Pennsylvania to see me. He said over and over, that he still loved me and I could hear it in his voice.

I had not laid eyes on Dan since that dreadful day on November eighteenth when I went to work. But even so, I knew that Dan loved me. I also knew that alcohol controlled him and that it changed him from a great guy to a monster. Like so many other women, I believed that our love was stronger than the alcohol and that I could change him.

This particular day was beautiful—warm and sunny and when Dan phoned me he asked if there was any way that I could go outside since he was banned from coming inside the rehab. center. Dan had driven all the way up from Florida to see me so of course I said yes.

I was thrilled at the thought of seeing Dan again. I wheeled myself outside the front doors of Harmarville Rehab and waited. When Dan arrived he got out of his car and sat on a bench next to my wheelchair. We talked for nearly an hour. He told me that he still had my engagement ring and couldn't wait for me to wear it again. He kept telling me how much he loved me and that he would do anything to have me back in his life again. He said, "I would just love to drive you away from here right now."

Meanwhile, I kept checking over my shoulder for fear that someone—a guard, a doctor, or one of my therapists to come looking for me.

Before he left, Dan kissed me and told me that he would be back for me.

When I got back to my unit, someone asked where I had been and I nonchalantly told them that I was in the gift shop and that was that.

May 31, 1987

Mom and I fought the entire time she was visiting me today. She accused me of being mentally ill because I told her that I wanted to be back with Dan. She said that I'm going to end up being put in a home. She was so mad at me that she left early. I was fit to be tied. She and Dean are being terribly mean.

I now understand that they were just trying to protect me. I wish I could have understood that at the time.

One of my favorite nurses, Marilyn, usually worked the midnight shift. One night she did something so funny that patients could hear me laughing in every part of the rehab. center. She was asking me what would be he first thing that I would do when I got home. I was using my hand signals to tell her that I would find myself a guy who was a ten. Marilyn knew exactly what my sign language meant and she laughed and said "stop it or I'll throw you in a cold shower!"

Once when we were talking about my restricted diet since I had trouble swallowing and had to be on pureéd food—Marilyn asked what I would eat first once I was at home and free to eat whatever I liked. I couldn't think of a motion for chocolate, so I typed it. Marilyn laughed and reached in her purse and handed me a piece of a chocolate candy bar saying, "Whatever you do, don't die. If you die eating this, I'll kill you!"

June 3, 1987

Thelma is still talking ninety miles an hour and I still cry just as much as she talks. I've just decided that I won't talk about Dan to anyone anymore. Let's see how long it will last. I have a one track mind. I have been so foolish, I thought Dan was the only man in the whole world for me.

June 6, 1987

Only four more days until I leave here! I can't wait. I have to come back for another year of out-patient therapy. I hope I get back to normal soon. Now that all of my in-patient therapy is over, I can say that Harmarville Rehab helped me a lot.

I keep expecting someone to tell me that I can't really go home for good. I went home for a visit again today and we had so much fun. We went shopping for more things to take with us when we go to visit Dean and his wife and daughter in Florida. It will be so wonderful not to be strapped in a wheelchair and have to follow all of these rules.

BACK HOME AGAIN
"OUR GOD REIGNS!"

June 10, 1987

Today is the day I leave here! I will follow-up with another year of out-patient therapy. I can hardly stand it, I'm so excited. More than that, Dom and I will be flying to Pensacola to see Dean!

As I was approaching the front desk and the doors to leave, the guard at the desk, whose name was Kevin, asked me for a date. I was so thrilled. I thought, maybe, just maybe I will get over Dan some day.

We did go out a few times and it was fun. But nothing ever came of it and we stopped seeing each other.

My brother, Dom escorted me out of the doors of Harmarville Rehab on the day of my release.

Immediately after leaving Harmarville, Mom and my Grandmother took Dom and me to the airport and we left for Florida to visit with Dean and his family.

JUNE 24, 1987

Dom and I are back after spending two weeks in Florida. It was so nice of Mom to send us on a vacation. Yeah, some vacation! Dean yelled at me most of the time, saying that I should be doing better than I was. If he wasn't yelling at me about my speech, he was yelling that I wasn't walking up to par, or he was criticizing my childish behavior. He wouldn't trust me to go up and down the stairs alone. He even had his four year old daughter, Jennifer trained to scream for him if I tried to manage the steps alone. It's pretty bad having a four year old watching out for me. But I now realize that Dean was just trying to protect me.

I keep thinking that I'm going to be going back to Harmarville to sleep and every time I realize that I don't have to live there anymore, I thank God.

I was released from Harmarville Rehab and within a couple of months, I was in bars again, dating, doing drugs, and always wanting to die. I wasn't able to drive so I went wherever people wanted to take me. I was always ending up in just another dark, smelly, smoky bar. I would ask myself, what am I doing in one of these places again? I don't belong here.

Drugs and alcohol were the reason Dan and I always fought. But I was in such a hurry to have a life again that I wasn't using good sense at all.

To make matters worse, no matter how crowded these places were, I always felt lonely and empty. I was crying inside for a miracle to free me from all of the self-destruction.

All the while I was still confessing everything I did to Mom. I couldn't stop myself. It was only later than I learned that this need to acknowledge and confess my sins was really the Holy Spirit working within me. It wasn't until nineteen ninety-two that I finally confessed again in church and received salvation.

August 13, 1987

On my way to therapy today, I saw what must have been my brother, Dean's twin. It was weird because he was even driving a car just like the one Dean owns. I was so excited, I thought Dean had come home for a visit. But it wasn't Dean although he did call me tonight. It was really nice to hear from him. He said that he was thinking about me all day today and that was especially nice to hear.

I had a good day at therapy today, too.

August 15, 1987

Today Mom and I went to the mall to get a pair of pants for Dom. She also bought me a really nice outfit. I don't know why, though. I don't have *anywhere* to wear it!

August 16, 1987

We went to my cousin Shawna's first birthday party today. We had a nice time.

August 17, 1987

I got up at six this morning and made Mom's lunch for work. I went back to sleep at eight and didn't get up until

Awake

noon. Then I laid out in the sun for an hour. Later, when I tried to jump from a step all by myself, I did it! I hope I can do it again tomorrow for Todd in physical therapy.

August 18, 1987

I wish I wouldn't have gone to therapy today. First, my social worker lectured me about Thursday night, flipping out like I did. (I had thrown a crying fit because Dan had kept calling me while Mom was at work last night. But Dom hung up on him every time so we never spoke.)

Then I got another lecture from Manny, my psychologist. I expected to hear something, but not that bad. To top it off Todd, my physical therapist wasn't there today. He can make me feel better just by smiling at me.

August 20, 1987

What a sickening day! Todd, the physical therapist that I like so much, had me in tears. He told another patient, "watch Rhonda let herself fall so that I have to catch her." I asked him why he said that and he said he'd rather not say. I started to cry and he said, "Rhonda, we can finish working or you can just leave now." I turned and left.

August 22, 1987

This is a rainy and dreary Saturday. It's boring. I think I'll go back to bed and sleep.

August 23, 1987

I slept until two-thirty in the afternoon and then I got up and had something to eat. Later Becky came by with this cute kid. Becky's been a really good friend—thank God. Later we went to my Aunt Eileen's house. It was neat because Mom let me drive up Eileen's driveway from the main road.

August 24, 1987

Same as always except that Roxanne, Dan's cousin drove by a couple of times yelling my name. This made Mom pretty mad.

August 25, l987
Today was another typical boring, bad day.

August 26, 1987
Mom was at work so I ate dinner alone and did the dishes. Aunt Carol will be driving me to therapy tomorrow since Mom will be working.

August 27, 1987
Therapy went alright.

August 28, 1987
Everyone told me that I looked nice today...including Todd! When I finally worked up the nerve to tell him how much I like him, it seemed like he didn't even care. He told me that he already has two girl friends and that we have to keep it a patient-therapist relationship. *I did not* want to hear this! I don't think I'll be able to face him again. I'm such a fool!

August 29, 1987
I just took a walk around the block a couple of times today. I was thinking about how it really feels like I died in the wreck and now I'm just floating around. Everything is *so different*. There's so much that I'm not able to do. Just as I've said a million times, I feel as if I'm watching some horror movie about a young girl who had her life turned inside out in a blink and had so much taken from her!

August 30, 1987
We went to the mall again so that Dom could get more school clothes. I got this really glamorous pink and silver dress. Maybe one day soon I'll get some sort of life back so that I'll be able to wear it. Mom bought me a jump rope so that I can practice.

August 31, 1987

Mom and I went food shopping. Then, a little while ago, she went to work. I'm dreading therapy tomorrow because Todd said we'll jump rope and I can't do it yet.

September 1, 1987

Manny, my psychologist, said that I'm doing really excellent. Manny said that my attitude has really improved over the weeks. He said my memory was sharp too. Of course I cried in Todd's class because I couldn't jump rope. Last week I could do it and now I can't. I don't' get it!

September 2, 1987

Today when I tried jumping, I could do it! Let's hope I can jump rope for Todd tomorrow.

September 3, 1987

Todd left early today for a meeting. Some other lady handled my therapy and I could jump for her! Maybe I'm trying too hard for Todd.

September 4, 1987

Todd said something to make me really mad today. He told me that maybe I'd better find myself a different teacher since I like him so much. I told him *no way*. I was furious! He better not be thinking about finding someone else to work with me!

September 5, 1987

I slept until two today when Becky called. Then we talked for awhile.

September 7, 1987

Mom worked today. I got up at noon and made her bed. After that, I did the dishes and practiced jumping rope for awhile. Then I wrote Dean a letter. It's his birthday today.

September 8, 1987

Mom was working again today. I woke up at one and did some cleaning. Tonight my right ear ripped open again. It was originally ripped in the accident. We went to the emergency room but they said they couldn't stitch it, that it would have to be done by a surgeon.

September 9, 1987

Today was depressing—nothing to do but cry. That drunken driver changed my life and he had no right! He should have to suffer like I am. I keep thinking that things will get better, but they never do.

I want to be able to walk and talk just like before and not like some two year old. I want to be able to pick up the phone and gab like I did before. I want to take long walks, I want to be able to get in the car and drive, or just take a bike ride and I can't do any of that! God couldn't have wanted me to live like this.

September 10, 1987

Today was awful. Manny told me I need to realize that I was in a very serious car accident and that people would always be able to tell that I had been through something traumatic. He made me feel so bad. I cried and cried. I really liked him until today. Fortunately, when I went to see Todd he was so charming and sweet. He made me feel much better

September 11, 1987

I'm all ready for Mom to take me for therapy at Harmarville. I didn't wake her yet, though. She worked all night.

I'm back from therapy. It went pretty well. Todd was in a really good mood again. I just dream about having someone like him.

September 12, 1987

Today was boring. I don't know why I'm so tired I haven't done a thing. You can tell how bad things are because I'm looking forward to therapy tomorrow. I'm going to bed now.

Awake

September 13, 1987

We went to my cousin, Melissa's birthday party today. When we got home Becky came and got me. We had lots of fun. I can't wait until the next time we go out.

September 14, 1987

No therapy today. I had an appointment at the University of Pittsburgh to get fitted for my palate lift. They took moulds of my mouth so that they can make the plastic lift that should elevate my palate so that my speech won't sound so nasal.

September 15, 1987

Mom and I signed papers today against Dan so that he can never come near me again. We also went to order me new contact lenses. I'm tired and going to bed now. I'll probably have nightmares because I am so mad at that man who hit me and caused all of this. The drunk is now suing my mother because she has legal guardianship. Is there no justice?

September 17, 1987

It rained all day and I was very bored. All I could think about was how boring my life is and how I never do anything fun anymore.

September 18, 1987

Today was okay. Mom and I picked up my new contacts. I was glad to get rid of those glasses. When I was at therapy Manny kept trying to get on my nerves. But I just kept laughing in his face. I wasn't going to let him upset me.

September 25, 1987

I talked to Paul from Recreation for about half an hour. He's pretty neat. I like him. Mom's at work so I'm lonely and bored.

September 26, 1987

It's about ten at night and Mom's going to work. I called a

friend from high school. His name is Bill. But he wasn't home so I talked to his mother for awhile. She said that Bill will probably call me back tomorrow night. But I doubt that after what I did to him on prom night. He's a nice guy and I now regret what I did. In fact I was calling him to apologize for ruining our prom night.

Bill was my prom date but I had already made plans with Dan to sneak out and drive off with him somewhere. I think we were planning to go to Seven Springs. But I got so drunk just before the prom. The reason I did that was I knew that Dan would be drunk when he picked me up and I wanted to be drunk too because I thought, if I can't beat him, then I'll join him. (I wish I would have known about Romans 8/8: *Those controlled by the sinful nature cannot please God.*) But I got so filthy drunk that I couldn't even walk straight. So Bill and I showed up at the prom and I smelled like a brewery and couldn't even talk. My General Business teacher had me immediately thrown out of the prom and an ambulance was sent to pick me up. I spent the night in the hospital and the doctor told my Mother that my heart had stopped twice. I remember smelling salts in my face and being forced to drink black stuff that was a lot like tar so that I would throw up—which I did, several times. So God has rescued me from death's door more than once.

September 27, 1987

Bill did call me back but he told me that he won't be able to call me back again. He said that his girlfriend is jealous (I didn't even know he had a girlfriend). I just hope he doesn't hate me for what I did to him prom night.

September 30, 1987

I went for a check-up today on my palate lift I told them that the dumb thing hurts too much for me to wear. I cried after I put it in because it hurt so bad. It felt like I was swallowing a chunk of glass.

They told me not to wear it if I can't stand the pain and I cannot!

October 1, 1987

Today in therapy, Bruce, my speech teacher, had me talking with my palate lift in! Several other speech teachers were called in to hear me speak and they all said that I sounded much better with it in. I think that it makes me sound worse! Anyone who tries talking with a mouthful of glass will definitely sound terrible!

October 2, 1987

I asked Jennifer, my Occupational therapist why I had to come to O.T. I saw no point in it. She said that the next time I go there she'll give me some really tough, on-the-spot questions and if I do well, I won't have to go to O.T. any more. Now I'm worried about how I'll do.

October 3, 1987.

Mom wanted me to go somewhere with her today but I didn't feel like getting dressed. Later I did get dressed and went with her to get food and a picture for the living room. I kept my palate life in for the hour that we were gone. It was quite uncomfortable. Mom and I went to the movies after shopping and that was nice. When we got home, I called my brother, Dean.

October 6, 1987

Today in therapy Todd told me that he knows that I'll be jumping rope by the time I'm done with therapy. Boy, I hope he's right. Well, he's the teacher, he must know what he's talking about.

October 7, 1987

Wow, what a day! It was unbelievable. Todd had me on the floor in therapy. I was on my hands and knees. He wanted me to kick my legs, one at a time. But I couldn't do it. In order to help me, he pulled my legs out from under me. That put too much weight on my hands and I fell flat on my face, smashing my nose on the cement floor. I thought that I broke my nose! Todd ran and called for an ambulance. So I was off to Saint

Margaret's hospital.

I was at the hospital from two in the afternoon until eight in the evening. But, thank God, I had no fractures though it felt as if I did.

My life is truly a soap opera. What a long day!

October 9, 1987

I thought I hated Todd after yesterday. But today I cried because I still have a crush on him. I know that he didn't mean to hurt me. He probably thought that I really could do what he wanted me to do. He may have even thought that I was faking when I said I couldn't do it. But I truly don't have the strength yet.

October 10, 1987

I thought things were bad enough but now they just got worse. I am so FURIOUS! I was just told that Todd is stepping down as my therapist. They said that he dismissed my case. Just like that!

October 20, 1987

Becky called late in the afternoon but I was asleep. I wish I could either learn to deal with this life of confusion and anger or just sleep my life away.

October 21, 1987

Mom called the administration at Harmarville and told them that she thought Todd was wrong to step down as my therapist. I guess I made his job pretty awkward. But he should know that some of my actions were due to my head injury and he should have been trained how to handle such things. The administrator told my Mother that he wants to meet with us to discuss the situation.

Oct 22, 1987

I didn't go to any therapy today. I don't ever want to go back, thanks to Todd. Mom's in bed and Dom went out somewhere. I hate how my life is shot to hell now. I never go anywhere but therapy. I don't have a boyfriend any more. I only have one friend, Becky, Carolyn doesn't come around anymore. I can't talk or walk right and I probably never will again. I wonder if the drunk who hit me ever stopped to think about how he changed my life...not that he would care.

OCTOBER 23, 1987

Mom and I went to Pittsburgh today to get me a second pair of contacts and get her a first pair of glasses. Then we went to pick up tickets to see David Copperfield at Heinz Hall.

OCT. 24, 1987

Mom, Dom, his friend, Roger and I all went to see this magician, David Copperfield, tonight. It was a wonderful show. Becky called and wanted me to go to bingo with her but I never feel like doing anything any more.

OCTOBER 25, 1987

Mom worked daylight today and I stayed home alone. When she got home we went to Dahlkemper's and she offered to buy me anything I wanted. How nice! I picked out a really pretty diamond marquise ring.

OCT 28, 1987

It's midnight and I can't sleep. Dean called tonight and said that he thinks my speech is getting better. That made me really happy. The rehab administrator called again and said he wants to meet with Mom and me this coming Monday. He's concerned because I haven't been going to therapy.

NOV. 2, 1987

We had our meeting today and Todd wasn't even there. The administrator said that he can't make Todd work with me. I'm sure someone has to be Todd's boss and that someone can make him! We're going to meet with Todd on Friday. That should be a lot of fun! I'm going to go to therapy tomorrow.

Nov. 5, 1987

I had a petty good day at therapy today. My occupational therapist told me that I did well with all the questions and now I don't have to go back to occupational therapy. This is good! When I walked into physical therapy Todd saw me and gave me a big smile and said "Hi, Rhonda!" I just turned my head and didn't say a word.

Nov. 7, 1987

I had the big meeting with Todd today. He only wanted to stay for five minutes. Mom let him know that she thought it was awfully rude of him to simply make an appearance and leave. So he stayed longer. I felt like crying again, but I held it in.

Nov. 8, 1987

I was feeling super-depressed and just cried all day. I kept having thoughts of suicide. Then I thought how Mom would get torn apart if I did something like that. She's going to go crazy either way because these mood swings that I have now are really horrendous. Besides, if I would try to overdose on my phenobarbitol, with my luck, I would just get sick. If I tried to slit my wrist, the knife would probably be too dull. This depression is really getting out of control. And just think, three selfish, heartless men are the cause of all this. First there is my dad who has never been there for me. Then Dan who used me for a punching bag when he couldn't handle his alcohol, which was more often than not. And finally, there is that driver in Florida who didn't consider the consequences of driving after having a few beers.

Nov. 10, 1987

Aunt Carol drove me to therapy today and I told Manny about how I was feeling—I told him about being suicidal and everything. It was a dumb move on my part because now he said he would have to get a psychiatrist involved in my case.

Nov. 12, 1987

I took a cab to therapy today. It was awful. First the driver was late. Then both the driver and the car stunk and the car seemed like it was going to blow up. I could go on but I'm too tired. Starting tomorrow, I have to go to Vocational for three hours.

Good night.

Nov. 13, 1987

The first thing I did in Vocational was get myself a cup of coffee. Patty, my teacher said that I did a good job and worked hard.

Nov. 15, 1987

This morning I cleaned out a kitchen cabinet, then I practiced running and then I walked down to Dom's friend's house with him.

Nov. 17, 1987

Today went pretty quickly. I practiced jumping rope, running and walking. Everyone tells me that I take really tiny steps and I need to take larger steps. They also tell me that I look stiff and that's because I'm afraid to swing my arms. I fear that too much motion will cause me to fall and I DO NOT want another head injury. I hope and pray that everything comes back to me naturally someday soon. Everything I do or try to do is such a big chore.

Nov. 18, 1987

My accident happened exactly one year ago today. I still can't comprehend any of this. I swear, it seems like I'm in a bad, bad dream. Only one more month until Christmas. I'm sure glad that I'll be home for Christmas this year!

One evening at about this time, I was in my bedroom at home in Springdale when I doubled over in pain. Mom called an ambulance and I was taken to the hospital. After many tests, I was diagnosed with chronic pancreatitis. The gastrointestinal specialist told me that while I was in a coma, my sphincter muscle forgot how to open wide enough for food to pass through.

Over a period of ten years, I would undergo four sphincterotomys to correct the problem. My doctor said that if these procedures didn't work, he might consider holding the muscle open with a stent. Finally, a temporary stent was placed in my pancreas. But over the next two decades, I would continue having attacks periodically with no permanent solution to the problem found to date.

The injuries from the wreck and subsequent coma have also resulted in my suffering chronic fatigue, and short term memory loss. I also have problems because my pelvis healed incorrectly while I was in a coma. This is causing my walking gait to be off with an exaggerated twist.

The close of 1987 gave me a lot to think about. What a year it had been! I had no memory of the end of 1986. I was told that in the last months of that year, I had been going to work with bruises and cuts all over my body from the beatings I was receiving from Dan. Then in November tragedy struck and I have no real conscious memories until the second month of 1987. After that, my year was filled with therapies, depression, and confusion.

1988

The holidays came and went and now it's a new year. I hope this one will be better.

I started my physical therapy with a new teacher. Her name is Pam and she's nice, but she's not Todd. I still see Todd around but I keep my emotions in control even though I miss him. I continue to go to physical therapy, psychology, and vocational. I can't wait to get done with all my therapy but it does give me something to do all day.

March 10, 1988

I turned twenty one today. Dean, his wife, and his daughter drove back home to help me celebrate. It was a nice birthday. Two of the local newspapers did very nice articles about me. They asked me all kinds of questions like, what it was like being in a coma, what I remember of it, and how I feel now. My Mom, brothers and I met with the reporters down at the health spa where I used to work out before I moved to Florida.

They had me pose with my brother helping me work out with weights. I loved it.

The article in the paper was really nice. But the reporter made a few mistakes. For example, it said that for my birthday my brother, Dean took me dancing, when, in fact, they took me to a comedy club because I like comedians and I couldn't dance anymore. The papers also said that I had less than a ninety-five percent chance of surviving when it should have read that I had a less than five percent chance of survival. The papers were also wrong when they said that I had scars on my face an hands as a result of the wreck. I thank God that that's not at all true! Luckily I only have my tracheostomy scar on my throat and a little scar on my right hand and a small one on my stomach. I am very grateful that no real physical damage was done. But I'm afraid that my emotions and behavior were messed up. I want so badly to be that normal nineteen year old girl that I was in November, 1986 before I left work on that terrible day.

I was very sad and depressed when my brother and his family went back to their home in Florida after their ten day visit. It was so wonderful to celebrate my birthday with all of my family but after they were gone, I just kept asking why me, *why me, why me,* back in the pitty-party mode.

The Harmarville Outreach Center, known as The Rock, was in a building located near the rehab center but not within walking distance. I was assigned to The Rock and spent six hours there in the morning and then took a shuttle bus over to the main facility for physical therapy and psychology in the afternoon.

The purpose was to get a patient to work on their strengths and weaknesses in order to get ready to work again. We were told that sometimes patients who complete the program get job referrals.

Sometimes we did computer work, sometimes we did worksheets or worked on math skills. Since I had nothing better to do, I didn't mind being at The Rock. But in the end it didn't result in my getting a job or even a job referral. It was, in the end a total waste of time, in my opinion.

This was the beginning of so many people telling me that there was nothing they could do to help me. I seemed to do so well with my physical recovery but no one seemed to be able to help me with my behavior and my emotional problems. I was always begging Harmarville for more help. Finally they referred me to Western Psych. Institute in Pittsburgh. I was to go there for one week of testing.

I was assigned a teacher by the name of Larry. He gave me more puzzles, tests and mind games that anyone could imagine. He video taped a practice job interview he had me do which brought some surprises.

Although I was nervous about how I would sound on the tape, when he played it back, I was pleased with the way I answered his questions. My voice was still pretty weak, but I did well with what I had to say. I answered the questions appropriately. Once in a while, I would slur a little. Sometimes I stuttered. I did hate hearing myself start to talk and having it come out sometimes jumbled and twisted like I was drunk. And I also watched for something Larry talked to me about. He said that I would hesitate when I was about to answer a question. Ever since coming out of the coma, it did take me longer to articulate my ideas and thoughts. I just had to think before I opened my mouth about what I wanted to say and how I wanted to say it. I never had to do that before or should have and never did.

The surprise to me was how pretty I looked. I watched the tape over and over and was really happy with the way I looked. That's something very strange about my experience. Now I appreciated my looks. I don't know if I was maturing or if God made me so grateful for my life that I was thankful for my whole physical being.

In the end, the more I watched and listened to my five minute interview, the more disappointed I was in how I sounded.

Along with making the tape, Larry also blindfolded me and had me do things with my hands. This frustrated me terribly and Larry told me that I would never be able to do

AWAKE

work with my hands. I would later learn that he was absolutely correct.

My social life was still nearly non-existent but then there was a glimmer of hope. At last I met someone nice at a party my younger brother, Dom had at our house. Bob was a year or two older than I was and we went out casually a few times. It wasn't that he was the love of my life but he was a nice guy and I did enjoy being with him and he seemed to like me.

I was sitting on the front steps of our house one beautiful, summer day in nineteen eighty-eight when Bob came by to show me his new car. So there we were, admiring his beautiful sports car when suddenly another car came flying down the hill. It turned the corner with tires screeching. Bob and I both remembered thinking, *that madman is going to smash into this beautiful new car.* Sure enough, the driver came flying right at Bob's new car and only missed hitting it by about an inch! Just as the car turned up from up the hill, I saw that the driver was Dan and I knew instantly that he was drunk. I felt my stomach ball-up into knots, my heart was racing and my knees were shaking. There was a horrible sound of screeching tires as Dan slammed on the brakes. We couldn't believe he had actually missed Bob's car. Bob and I stood there in utter shock as Dan got out of his car and staggered up to me.

"Rhonda baby, if you ever loved me at all, you won't say anything against me. Do you hear?" He was referring to a summons he had received to appear in court. Apparently, my mother had filed a restraining order to have Dan kept away from me, as she was my legal guardian at the time.

By this time Mom had heard the racket outside and looked out the window. I don't think there is anyone she hated more than Dan and she couldn't call the cops fast enough. They were at the scene in no time and it was a circus—four cops, drunken Dan who couldn't even walk straight. Bob and Dan screaming in each other's face, pushing each other—about to get into a slug fest.

To make matters worse, Dan's mother and older sister suddenly came tearing down the hill. When they caught sight of me they yelled, "Rhonda, it's is all your fault!"

They apparently felt that Dan was drunk and upset because of the restraining order which was, of course, filed on my behalf.

Since Dan was obviously drunk and at fault, he was handcuffed and shoved into the back of the police car. It broke my heart when he looked up at me as they were taking him away and said, "Baby, don't let this happen!"

I thought, "Dan, why don't you see that you are the one who's letting it happen every time you get drunk! And as for me—how could I still love you when I know you'll never, ever quit drinking."

Bob left, Dan went to jail and I went to my room to cry again.

Mom came in and asked why I was crying so hard. I told her that I didn't understand why my life had to change so much all because of that wreck. I wanted to know why I had to be in a coma. Why did I still love Dan? And why don't I ever get any answers to my questions?

My Mother wanted desperately to get me as far away from Dan and his family as possible. So in October of 1988, she found another house in another town and announced to Dom and me that we were moving. Though we would just be moving a short distance away, apparently Mom felt it would make a difference for me. Mom said that this house would be better for me being that it was a raised ranch house and didn't have as many steps. But I knew that the main reason that we were moving was to get me away from Dan and his family.

Though she had my best interest at heart, my Mother succeeded not only in getting me away from Dan but from my best friends as well. The three girls I was closest to in high school, aside from Becky, were gone from my life. They were the ones Mom had banned from the rehab. center because, she said, they were talking about things they shouldn't have at my bedside while I was still comatose.

Christmas of 1988 would be our first in our new house. Mom, Dom and I decorated to the hilt and with the snow that fell that year, our new home looked like a house on a Christmas card.

Dean and his family came home for the holidays and it was

wonderful, but as always, when they left, I was very depressed.

I kept fantasizing about calling Dan and us riding off together. This actually did happen twice since the accident. The first time was when I was still going to out-patient therapy. I had been walking from class to class daydreaming about him, so I stopped a gave him a call. He sounded so happy to hear from me. He begged me let him pick me up. At first I told him that I absolutely could not leave the rehab center in the middle of therapy. In the end, that is exactly what I did with the stipulation that he have me back at exactly three o'clock when my Mom would be picking me up.

It felt weird being with him again. It had been two years since we were last together. I was nervous and it felt awkward. Dan kept telling me how great I looked and that he wished I would marry him because he loved and missed me so much.

We drove to a nearby park and talked for only half an hour. He had me back at the rehab on time and Mom never found out.

I didn't see Dan again until the following year. I was laying out in the sun in our backyard. Mom was working and Dom was out. Dan came driving through our alley and stopped when he saw me. He was really taking a chance by stopping because he couldn't have known that Mom wasn't at home. Again he begged me to take a ride with him. Then he reached in his pocket and said, "I have something for you, Rhonda." It was my engagement ring. He pleaded with me to take the ring back and say that I would still marry him. This was all I needed to add to my torment and confusion! But on that sunny day, I resisted and sent Dan on his way. I knew if I went anywhere with him that Mom and Dom would find out and send a search party out looking for me.

If I had to be in that horrible car crash, why did I have to awaken from the coma into this crazy life with a dad who wouldn't even come to see me on my death bed and a fiancé who drank and beat me.

As Dan's birthday, August eleventh, was approaching I kept telling myself that I had the perfect excuse to call him and wish him a happy birthday. I told myself that if I called him, it would absolutely be the last time. I was seeing a counselor at Mental Health at this time and she told me that if I was ever going to get over Dan, I needed to write down everything that concerned me about him.

In the end, all of this made me realize that Dan would never change. But as this conviction began to grow, it was God who really opened my eyes and carried me through everything. But I wasn't aware of this just yet because my journey was only beginning.

"I know the plans I have for you, not to harm you, but to give you hope and a future." - Jer. 29:11

I can't think of a lonelier time in my life than after my accident. I no longer had a fiancé, friends, or even co-workers. I felt so very alone. I thought the loneliness was going to kill me. This is when my brother's dog became my dog and my one true friend. I used to hate the isolation that I felt and Daisy Mae would give me comfort the best way she could. She was a great companion.

But I still desperately needed human companionship. And I needed to be with people my own age. I felt so lost that I even asked our neighbor if she knew anyone my age that I could be friends with.

Amazingly, she told me about this girl named Carol. She said that Carol had a disease called scoliosis, which caused her to be only about four feet tall.

I used to feel as if I had a disease too. When people hear that you have a head injury, they treat you differently. For one thing, they talk very slowly as if I wouldn't be able to comprehend otherwise. Or they would talk very loud, as if I were deaf!

I can just imagine what this girl had to endure growing up with a real disease. I knew that I could relate to her but then I thought we wouldn't have anything in common. And I was sure we would never have an opportunity to meet.

But it turned out that this girl, Carol, has sent some brochures to my neighbor for me to read over. They were brochures about a Christian singles group that she belonged to.

AWAKE

When I thought about a singles group, I thought no one would ever want to date me again. I can't imagine anyone wanting to be with me after I had gone through so much trauma and loss. I had a speech impediment, mixed-up emotions, problems controlling my bladder, and no job. Who would ever want me?

I can't remember now, who called who, but I remember thinking how nice and polite she was on the phone. Soon we had made plans to go to a singles meeting in Oakland. It was amazing how friendly everyone was. And I couldn't believe that I was seeing people actually having fun without being in a bar. I watched one really good-looking young guy singing and praying and I thought, *I can just see Dan going to a group like this, reading from the Bible, and praying out loud. Ya right, never in a million years!*

After the meeting, Carol and I went to get something to eat. Being with her I wasn't apprehensive at all. I was relaxed and had a great time. She was telling me how she learned not to judge people. I remember thinking, *she's talking from experience. She had to deal with much criticism while growing up, especially from kids who didn't know better.*

About a month after we first met, Carol and I signed up for a class at a nearby high school. The class, which was every Tuesday for six weeks, was on co-dependency. I thought that the class might help me since I was still so hung-up on Dan.

I learned that this kind of dependency was likely to happen if, as a child, you missed the love and support from one parent, as I always did. My Mother was always there for me, but not my dad—not ever.

Carol and I never missed a class. We were learning a lot and we enjoyed it. But sometimes I enjoyed it too much and nearly got us kicked out with my laughing. It happened during class when one of the students got up to go to the rest room. When she returned and attempted to sit down, the chair pinched her leg. Now I'm not proud of this but, at the time, this was enough to set me off laughing. To make matters worse, the girl kept whimpering and making remarks about her leg, and the more she did it the harder I laughed.

In the meantime, Carol, who sat in front of me, was trying

to ignore me. I knew what she was doing and why so I honestly tried to control myself. But the more I tried, the funnier it got and the more I laughed and laughed. Now I wasn't going to put this in my book, but it ended up that I laughed so hard that I wet my pants. It may not be a pretty picture, but it's the truth about the things I had to deal with since my head injury. At least this time, I got a good laugh out of it. Other times I cried like a baby.

Another time, Carol and I were in a restaurant cracking-up over something and soon I lost control and my pants, the chair, and the floor were soaked. I started crying and Carol just didn't know what to do. So I told her to call my Mother.

Mom came right over and took me home. But when I got in the car she said, "Now Rhonda, after everything you've been through, you're going to have to concentrate a lot harder than other people so that this doesn't happen."

I felt like such a "freak-a-zoid!" There I was, suddenly awake from this coma facing so many unwanted changes. It was like being hit in the face with a ton of bricks. I remembered back in rehab. when I would ask 'When will I be better? When will I have any sort of life again? They would always answer with 'in time.' But I felt how about NOW or YESTERDAY!

When Carol took me to her Christian singles group in Pittsburgh, she told me that I'd surely meet a nice guy there. I didn't believe her but I went anyway On the way down she told me about a physician and a dentist who both attended the group meetings. She said that her friend was dating the doctor. So I said, "You just watch, that dentist won't want to have anything to do with me."

I was wrong. As soon as we got there and sat down, I noticed this tall, good-looking man staring at me. He eventually worked his way over and introduced himself as Jon. As we were talking, he asked if I planned to go with the group on their upcoming camping trip the next week. I told him that I didn't know anything about it, but that I might consider going.

Jon seemed really interested in me and later I found out that he was the dentist that Carol had told me about! Now if I could just get enough nerve to go on this camping trip, I thought I might have a lot of fun. Jon had said that the group was going to be spending the weekend camping at Ohio Pyle—this beautiful spot along a river, in the mountains, about two hours from Pittsburgh.

When I went home that night, I excitedly told Mom about my evening—the people I had met and the dentist who had asked me to go along of a camping trip with the group. Mom was happy that I was actually getting out and meeting people. She even called Jon and told him that I would be joining the group on their trip.

I was a little nervous about the trip because I had never been camping before and Carol wasn't going. But the next weekend, Mom drove me to the church in Oakland where we all met for the trip to Ohio Pyle. I felt strange not really knowing anyone. But they were all friendly and put me at ease.

Overall, it was a fun weekend of hiking, canoeing, and singing songs around a camp fire. And I surprised myself by really liking the whole thing since I'm not really an outdoors kind of girl. I enjoyed the hiking and boating most of all. And over the course of the weekend, I learned all I needed to know about Jon the dentist. I found out that he was a big phony. There was one girl on the trip who turned out to be his girlfriend of seven years! And still, every chance he got, behind every rock and tree, Jon was coming on to me.

The trip taught me a few things like not to be so trusting and to remember that—church-goer or not—people may not be what they seem.

I know that it was God's will that Carol came into my life when she did. I was so very lonely and she was the new friend that I really needed. All of my old friends were gone. Becky was working and living out of state. Carolyn was busy with her boyfriend, Scott, whom she eventually married. My old life was gone and I didn't know it then but I had a brand new life about to begin.

Once I was out of therapy, I went out to bars a few times to try to get my old life back. Now I wish that I had skipped all of that foolishness. But when I would start to feel anxious and impatient, I would go out and do stupid things believing that I was taking control of my life. I didn't know then that if I would have just waited for God, things would have been handled perfectly. Now I know that prayer and patience can do so much more for you than anything or any one else. But at the time, I tried everything to make things happen my way. I just didn't understand that God had a plan for me with everything all worked out.

I went to many singles meetings, to clubs, and bars trying to find that special person. I feel like such a fool now and I know that God must have been thinking, *"Rhonda, when you get done with those petty things, I will go to work for you, but not until then."*

One weekend Carol and I went to another singles meeting in Oakland and there I was introduced to a very good looking guy. He seemed interested in me right away. When a group of us decided to go out to get something to eat, he asked me to ride with him. I was impressed by his beautiful, blue Corvette and his excellent manners. Before the evening was over, he asked for my phone number and two days later, he called me to ask me out on a date.

Our date was perfect. He took me to dinner, then to a movie. We went for this wonderful trolley ride and had fun window shopping. He was easy to talk to and he told me that he was thirty-five and was self-employed. Over the next month, we went out many times and I came to realize that he truly was a good Christian man—not anything like the first guy I met.

But as much as I liked him, I lost him when he learned that I had not been saved. "Rhonda," he told me, " "you need to find God before you can find the right man." He went on to explain that he was looking to marry a Christian woman.

I was mad, ashamed and hurt. But I would learn that he was right—though it took me some time to do that. He was more or less telling me that I needed to *"Come near to God and He will come near to you."* - James 4:8

On July fourth, my Mom and I went to the Springdale football field to watch fireworks. I kept looking around, hoping that I'd see Dan there. I felt so sad and jealous seeing all of the young couples together, laughing and carrying on. I kept thinking that I used to be like them. *I used to have a boyfriend. Now I'm here with my mother.* I hadn't yet reached the point in my spiritual growth where I could be grateful that I had my mother to enjoy things with. Instead I just sat there feeling sorry for myself. Then I got it into my head to go to the club where I used to work. At first Mom didn't want to go to W.P. Nix, but I begged and begged and she finally agreed.

Once we got there I again felt out of place and sad seeing everyone dancing and having fun. I had to fight to hold back the tears. Then, when a slow song came on, a guy asked me to dance. *"Please God, let me still be able to at least slow dance!"*

My prayer was answered. And my partner, his name was Joel, seemed like a nice guy. Before we left, Joel asked for my phone number. He called me the next day and we went to a carnival and for a ride. The next night Joel picked me up and took me to his parents' house. It was a beautiful house. Joel told me his father was a doctor. He had such good manners and even though he wasn't a Christian, I could tell he was a nice person. But I apparently stilled needed to do a lot more work on my own character. It wasn't long before I wrecked my relationship with Joel because of my immature behavior.

When I first awoke from the coma, I felt hopeless and sad but the severe depression that would descend upon me would come later. In the beginning I had no control over my emotions. I would laugh hysterically at almost anything and often at the most inappropriate times. Then, just as often, I would burst into tears and cry for hours at a time. I knew that this behavior wasn't rational, but I couldn't control myself. It was as if my brain forgot the difference between right and wrong.

Even before the accident, I was a person of intense emotions. Now, since I had suffered a head trauma, everything that was happening to me was extreme.

I would go out to dinner with my Mother and brother and something would set me off laughing hysterically. Once I started, there was no stopping me. I would laugh until I wet my pants and then I would be so upset at wetting my pants that I would cry for hours.

How I hated that four-letter word, TIME! *Now Rhonda, you just have to give it time.* Time had been taken from me and everyone was asking me to just sit back and wait while more time passed.

My mood swings finally did improve. But in the two years after my accident, I focused more and more on my limitations. I refused to be thankful for surviving the terrible crash. I could only concentrate on the losses of my life.

By September, 1988 I had completed all therapies, testing and classes. It was good to be done with everything but I was terrified. *My God, what do I do now?* I had no job, no skills, no talents. I was so scared about my future. Yes, the therapists had done their job getting me to walk and talk again but now it felt as if they were just throwing me out into the world without a clue.

But before I even left the rehab, God allowed something else to happen that gave me some encouragement.

Just as I was turning the corner in the hall at rehab, I ran into a friend from high school. He looked like he was seeing a ghost as he said, "Rhonda, is that really you? I cannot believe that you're alive!"

He explained that he had contributed to my accident fund but he somehow thought that I had passed away.

After we talked awhile, he invited me to go to a rock concert with him to see my favorite group, "Guns-n-Roses." We went to the concert on Halloween night and I had a wonderful time. But as good as that was, I felt I needed some kind of occupation and at that time, I truly believed that that would never happen.

I wished I could just snap my fingers and evaporate!

I celebrated my twenty-first birthday with my family.

My sister-in-law, Liza, niece, Jennifer, and brother, Dean came up from Florida for my birthday.

The evening of my twenty-first birthday, Dean and Liza took me out to a comedy club.

OFF THE DEEP END

I HAD COME a long way by the third year after my coma. But I was always expecting more of myself. I thought I should have been driving by then. I wanted to be able to talk better and I wanted to get a job. There was this huge emptiness in my life that made me restless and dissatisfied.

One day I saw something in the newspaper about night classes. When I mentioned this to my Mother she was supportive and offered to go with me to see the school and be interviewed.

Once we got there, the interviewer began to stress the idea of my becoming a full-time day student. Night classes were discouraged. When I mentioned that I wouldn't be able to get to school on a full-time basis, a woman in the room who overheard the conversation stepped in and said that she would be happy to pick me up every day and bring me home.

At first, I wanted nothing to do with being a full-time student again—ride or no ride. But as the interviewer spoke, I thought about how proud Mom and Dean would be of me. I wanted so much to impress them that I began to warm to the idea.

When we got home, we phoned Dean and he was so excited to hear about my plans. He suggested I study to become a medical assistant. That meant I would be taking an eighteen month course with classes held Monday through Friday from nine in the morning until three in the afternoon. I could tell that Dean was impressed and so I decided to do it.

In July of nineteen eighty-nine, I started classes. From the very first day, I felt intimated, especially by the people in the class who were much older than I was. But I kept telling myself, *I'm just as smart as they are and I'll do just as good.* I wish that had been the case. But what I couldn't or wouldn't admit was that none of these people had suffered a head injury and that meant they did have a big advantage over me.

One day one of the students recognized me from an article that had been in the local newspaper. Word spread quickly and soon I was getting lots of sympathy and pity but no real friendship. Only one girl in the class, Denise, would talk to me and I appreciated her kindness. But I felt like some kind of freak walking around. I knew that other people were staring at me and whispering.

Once I overheard a girl who was sitting behind me say, "They better slow down or Rhonda will be lost."

At first I thought, *your ignorance will make me stronger and better.* And it did. I got two A's and two B's. Mom was proud, Dean and Dom were proud and I was too. But I should have known it was all too good to last.

I loved medical terminology and all of the new things I was learning until we had to start doing things with our hands. I was a disaster when it came to taking blood pressures or doing anything physical. Then, it seemed all of my abilities began to fail me. It was as if I was blind, deaf and dumb. I'd be sitting in class, the teacher would be talking away and everyone would be taking notes and there I'd be still trying to comprehend the first thing the teacher had said.

I couldn't keep up.

I was getting more and more depressed—always dwelling on the things that I couldn't do—not able to handle the pressure of trying to be like everyone else in school. I was assigned a counselor and a psychiatrist and I saw each of them every week.

On the evening of March seventeenth of nineteen ninety I went to an appointment with my psychiatrist. This was to be my last session with him but little did I know it was just the beginning of something far worse than I had yet endured.

As I was talking with him that evening I was being my usual honest self, telling him exactly what was going on and how I felt. He let me talk for a while then he said, "Well Rhonda, this has been put off for too long. You need to go somewhere."

"What do you mean I need to go somewhere?" I asked. "I absolutely cannot go anywhere! I might think I'm behind now but if you make me miss even one day, it will all be over with for me at school!"

The doctor told me that he understood but he said that he had no choice.

I begged and pleaded with him not to make me go

anywhere. But he kept telling me that his mind was made up and that this was for my own good.

I tried to assure him that I would not hurt myself. But he apparently didn't believe me. I told him I had things to do. I had commitments. I was supposed to model some clothes in a fashion show at school. And that day after that I had a doctor's appointment. But he wasn't listening to me any more.

At first I was laughing in disbelief. Then I cried hysterically. It reminded me of when I first came out of the coma. I didn't have control of my emotions or my facial expressions. Often I would laugh or cry at the most inappropriate times. I overcame that but here I was again.

When the ambulance crew came into the doctor's office to take me to the psychiatric ward of Forbes Regional Hospital, I recognized one of them as the reporter who had interviewed me about my accident. She gave me a hug and said "Oh Rhonda, it's you!"

I was glad to have someone I knew ride with me. On the way to Forbes she told me that she hoped I wasn't assigned to this one particular doctor who she said was mean and creepy.

Can't you just guess who was assigned to my case! But it turned out that this doctor was not the monster he had been described as being. He was soft-spoken, peaceful and very calm. And, as time went on, I grew to idolize this man.

I was in the hospital for a total of five weeks. During that time, I asked to see a minister. I had planned to ask him to perform an exorcism. That's how depressed and confused I was. I believed I was possessed by the devil. I felt as if I was sinking lower and lower. It got so bad that I was having thoughts that I would be better off dead.

At last the day came when Reverend Josten arrived. I will never forget the feeling I had when I met him. He stayed and talked with me for two hours. He shook my hand as he was leaving and gave me this big, godly smile. It was really a great feeling. I was so calm and happy with him. I wished he could stay forever.

Once I realized that I had a wonderful doctor and a wonderful minister, my hospital stay didn't seem so bad.

While in the hospital I met many people. All of them were

AWAKE

very troubled. There was a guy in the room next to mine who talked to himself all of the time. I would watch him pacing back and forth carrying on these intense conversations. Though he could be pretty hostile with a lot of the other people. He was always very nice to me. One day, however, he came up to me and announced that I was his common law wife. He said that he had paced off the number of steps between his bed and my bed and, according to his measurements, we were man and wife. This was the first of my many crazy experiences in the hospital.

I don't know if it was because I was lonely or because I missed having a dad but my admiration for my doctor and for the minister grew into really big crushes. I would imagine being married to one of them and having the other as my dad. They both knew that I was very fond of them.

On my last day in the hospital, Rev. Josten came in to see me. We talked and prayed and he asked me to come and visit his church. I told him that I would love to attend his church but that I didn't have any way of getting there. Then he looked at me with those wonderful eyes and made me feel as if he really cared for me. He told me that he had already taken care of that and that a friend of his would be coming to pick me up for services and would bring me home.

I did attend Reverend Josten's church for a few months and met a lot of wonderful people there. But my old demons came back and I soon found myself in trouble again.

Since being forced to leave school, I was so bored and lonely. Every week, when I'd meet with my counselor, I would tell her how depressed I was about having no direction.

My counselor urged me to go to a center in Pittsburgh that she said would train me and help me find a job. She was so enthusiastic about this place that she convinced me to go.

The following Monday I moved into the small guest house near the institute where I would be staying. I was feeling very positive about the place and after dinner I took a walk around the block, enjoying my freedom.

When I returned I found that I had a roommate. As she unpacked, she chatted with me and she seemed nice enough. She said that her husband was downstairs and she was going down to join him.

I had settled down to write letters to Mom and Becky when the woman came back and asked me if I would like to come downstairs to visit with her and her husband. I thought she was just being thoughtful and friendly, so I went.

It wasn't long before I regretted my decision because the woman was going on and on about all of her miscarriages and abortions—telling details that I, as someone she just met, should not have been told. When I had had enough of her personal history, I told them that I had to finish my letters and I went back upstairs. I was lying on my bed, not quite asleep, about an hour later, when the woman came up and without saying a word, took her pillow and left.

The next morning when I woke up, I saw that my roommate's bed had not been slept in. As I was brushing my teeth, the woman who ran the rehab asked me to come over to her office right away.

When I got there, there were two women in the office and they asked me to have a seat while they explained to me that they knew everything about what was going on with me.

"Good," I answered, "now tell me 'cause I don't know."

It was then that they told me that I wouldn't be staying at the institute. They explained that my roommate had been in to warn them that I was planning to hang myself in my room! She told them that she was so worried about me that she even snuck my bottle of Prozac out of my dresser drawer in the middle of the night.

The two women said that they had already called for a taxi to take me home. I pleaded with them to hear the truth. I told them that this woman was lying. I cried and begged them to let me stay. I could feel myself getting sick and depressed again. But they wouldn't let me talk and soon I was crying and shaking.

They escorted me to the guest house to get my things. And before I knew it, the taxi was there to get me and I was on my way home. Instead of a three week stay, I had lasted only twenty-four hours.

Within a week I was back in the hospital again. This time it was the psych ward. My counselor had suggested I go and since I had done so voluntarily, I only stayed two days before I signed myself out.

Things only got worse for me at home. I knew that I'd be hurting myself if I didn't let someone know. I had great trust for my doctor from Forbes Regional so I called him.

Dr. Stanger arranged for me to be admitted to a local hospital he also practiced in and I can honestly say that this time I actually enjoyed the stay.

My roommate at this hospital was a pretty, young girl who had many problems—just like me. Another of the patients, a young man named Norman also became a close friend of mine. Norman was only twenty-two. He was soft-spoken and shy. And from the beginning he followed me everywhere.

I left the hospital before Norman did and when I was being wheeled out to the ambulance on a stretcher, he rushed over to give me a hug good-bye. He slipped a noted into my hand and told me not to read it until I got into the ambulance.

The note started out with him telling me how much he loved our brief friendship. He told me how easy it was for him to talk to me. He said that he had told me things that he had never told anyone. He wrote his phone number and told me to call him whenever I could.

The reason I was leaving this hospital was that my Mother wanted me to go to a place called the Allegheny Neuropsychiatric Institute (it was called ANI for short.) Mom had heard about ANI and was very enthusiastic about it. She told me that this wasn't just another hospital but a facility that deals specifically with head injuries. She told me that they would be able to determine the cause of my depression. So how could I not give it a try.

On the day that I was being transferred, I was lying there in the ambulance I was thinking, *Here I go again. Will this craziness ever stop?*

From the beginning I didn't have a good impression of ANI. I arrived at ANI on a Friday and didn't meet my doctor until Monday. When he came in he immediately started pushing the idea of drugs. When he mentioned that his wonder drug was Lithium I said, "No way! Forget it." But he asked me to think it over. A few days later, we worked out a deal. I told him that if he got me out of recreational and occupational therapy, I would try his drug. He agreed and soon they were on their way to turning me into one of their zombies. And that's no exaggeration. When you looked around the unit I was in, all you saw were depressed patients walking around looking like the walking dead.

Before I met my doctor, a guy came to see me and introduced himself as my social worker. I decided that I didn't like him after I said, "I need to talk to you whenever you have time." And he answered, "Not now, Rhonda, I don't have time!"

Since I was a head injury patient and not always able or willing to control what came out of my mouth, I was so hurt that I yelled obscenities at him for about ten minutes.

As time passed, I came to respect one of the doctors who was working with me but I was still having a lot of problems. Though I was on nine different drugs including Lithium, it seemed that my depression was deepening. I was obsessed with the devil and with dying. I was having morbid visions and hearing voices. But after five weeks at ANI, without any warning, the staff began packing my things and getting me ready to ship back to the hospital I had come from!

I felt so helpless. No one would answer my questions and when I saw my doctor standing by the elevator, as I was being wheeled out, he took my hand and said, "Good luck, Rhonda. I like you a lot."

I prayed that Dr. Stanger, back at the hospital, would be able to help me. I prayed for a miracle. I didn't know at the time that the only one who could bring about a miracle was He who created us.

As usual, I was crying my eyes out as the ambulance came to take me on the hour-long drive back to Allegheny Valley Hospital. But when I returned my two friends, Jenny and Norman were gone. I feared that neither one went home.

I did learn later that Jenny had broken a light bulb and slit her wrists and that earned her a trip to the state hospital. I couldn't believe that Dr. Stanger would do that to her. She wasn't crazy, she was just sad.

I never did learn what happened to Norman. He had sent

cards to me at ANI but he never put a return address on them. I tried calling him many times. But there was never an answer. Then one day, a woman picked-up and angrily told me that Norman did not live their any more.

It was so sad not to be able to get in touch with Norman or Jenny. I wanted so much to try to help them. Meanwhile, I couldn't seem to do anything to help myself.

As soon as I was back in Dr. Stanger's care, he took me off the Lithium and everything else.

Christmas 1990 was approaching and Dr. Stanger told me that my insurance would not allow me to be able to go home on an overnight visit for the holiday. A twelve-hour pass was the best he could do.

As happy as I was that day when Mom came to get me for my nine a.m. to nine p.m. holiday, I was also afraid to leave the hospital. I knew how sick I was and all I kept thinking was how much I hated the world and all the people in it. No matter where I was or what I was doing, I was always trying to come up with ways to kill myself. I even considered walking in front of a moving car.

In spite of this, things went well at home. Mom and Dom were both trying hard not to upset me. But I watched and waited for them to make a mistake so that I would have an excuse to blow up and kill myself. I had even sneaked into Mom's bathroom and taped a razor blade to the inside of my sweater to use later.

As the time approached for Mom to take me back to the hospital, I asked her if she would take me to the K-Mart to buy some shampoo. She did and I took the opportunity to run in, buy the shampoo and steal some more razor blades. I stole them because I thought I'm sure not going to pay for something that I'm going to use to kill myself.

I stuffed some of the razor blades in my coat pocket and some in my shoe. I knew Mom would check my bag.

Once back at the hospital with Mom I was both mad that I had to be there and glad to be back inside and away from the big, ugly world.

Mom kept looking at me. Finally she said, "Come on, Rhonda. What do you have and where do you have it?" She said she could tell because I was walking stiffly.

I was amazed.

First she found the one in my sweater. Then she found the packet of razors in my coat pocket. I still had one in my shoe. But now Mom was off to the nurse's desk yelling, "Look what I found on my daughter! Why wasn't she checked when she came in?"

When Mom came back into the room she ordered me to give her anything else I might have hidden. I swore to her that I didn't have a thing and she stormed out of the room.

I thought that she had left for the night so I kicked the last razor out of my shoe. I kept telling myself *You have to do it now, Rhonda. Just be quick and get it over with.* These were not voices I was hearing as the doctor's kept suggesting. It was just my subconscious mind with goofy, destructive thoughts.

I started slicing away but I wasn't even smart enough to cut my wrists. When you get as depressed as I was, you aren't thinking straight and that's why it's hard to succeed. I cut my forearms. I even ran the blade across my throat a couple of times. But my skin seemed too tough to cut. I thought I would cut my juggler vein but even that wouldn't work for me. I was still trying to cut myself and there was blood everywhere when Mom walked back in.

> "God is our refuge and strength, an ever present help in time of trouble." - Psalms 34:1

She immediately called for help and suddenly the room was filled with people. They took the blade from me, wrapped my wounds, put me in a wheel chair and rushed me to the emergency room.

By the grace of God, not one of my wounds was even deep enough to require stitches. But on that night, I had no gratitude in me. When Dr. Stanger walked in, I attacked him.

"What are you doing here! Just go back to your happy family, your happy dog, your happy cat, your happy kids and finish sipping your hot chocolate by the fire place, like I'm sure you were doing!"

If I had known or understood what my actions were going

to get me, it might have shaken me out of this terrible cycle. But I was ignorant of the consequences and so I was stunned when on December 31st, my hero, Dr. Stanger sent me away for a ninety-day stay at the state mental hospital. That was some New Years Eve!

I know now that my shouting at him in the emergency room was merely my jealousy toward anyone who had the normalcy in life that I had lost and so desperately needed.

But it wasn't Dr. Stanger who told me I was going to be sent away, it was his partner, whom I disliked. Dr. Stanger had gone off on a holiday ski vacation when this doctor, coldly announced to me that I would be going to the state hospital for the new year. All during my treatment, I did my best to avoid ever seeing this doctor. Whenever I would be forced to talk with her, she would always tell me that I was a very sick girl. That was in marked contrast to Dr. Stanger who always took a positive approach and told me that he thought I was getting better.

Of course I cried and I begged and I cried some more, but nothing made any difference. I was going to the state mental hospital—the nut house where they sent crazy people—and there was nothing anyone could do about it.

I now know that I needed to begin claiming some of the Lord's promises.

> "The Lord is my rock, my fortress and my deliverer. My God, my rock in whom I take refuge, my shield and the horn of my salvation. My stronghold." - Psalms 18:2

The nurses were so kind to me when they heard I was being sent away. A couple of them said, "Now Rhonda, just prepare yourself. Even the day you're being wheeled out of here, just keep strong and keep smiling as hard as it will seem."

But I thought *no way I can smile unless God Himself goes with me to that horrible place!*

Well, it seems that God Himself did accompany me. I was able to leave A.V.H. with a smile on my face and I waved good-by to everyone with dignity .

Once I arrived at that hell-hole that passes for a hospital, I was shown to a room that had three other beds. That's nice, I was going to have three crazy roommates! -

> *"I am in pain and distress, may your salvation, Oh God, protect me."* - Psalms 69:29

Next you lose your privacy and dignity when a staff member makes you undress, shower and rub medication all over your body. This is to prevent scabies and the staff member watches you closely throughout the whole embarrassing procedure!

It was like I was a prisoner in a penitentiary.

When this first ordeal was over, I went to a pay phone to call Mom. "How did I ever end up here! I don't belong here! I'm not crazy!" I said over and over through my tears.

Back in my room, where the door always had to be open, a young man who introduced himself as Bill, stopped in to ask why I was crying.

"I'm in here. Isn't that enough reason to cry?"

He then asked me to go to the day room with him. I forced myself to go along. When I got there, I noticed that Bill and I were the only two normal-looking people there. There was one man in a corner of the room who looked to be in his thirties. He was just sitting in a wheel chair staring into space. Every once in a while he would drop his head and foam would come out of his mouth. I learned that every day, he would be wheeled into this corner and left to sit there until bedtime. Aides would come to feed him but other than that, he had no life at all. I noticed that he never even left the spot to go to the restroom. I suppose they had a diaper on him.

How was this helping him? How could this happen? And how was being in this place going to help me? It was like being in a horror movie.

I was feeling so sorry for myself and I began to think that I needed to talk to Dan. So I made another stupid mistake and I went and called him.

When he answered the phone, Dan sounded very happy to

hear from me. He said he'd come out to visit as soon as he found out how to get there. He told me how much he loved me and that's just what I wanted to hear. Then I heard voices in the background laughing and talking.

"Who's there?" I asked.

"Just a few of my friends," Dan said.

"He's lying!" I heard a female voice say—then laughter.

I hung-up angry and hurt. *How could Dan be laughing and having fun when I'm going through this hell!*

I was back to my room crying when all three of my roommates came in. I didn't say a word to any of them as I got ready for bed. One of the women was about thirty-five years old and was covered with burns. I never knew her name. The other, Cindy, was about forty and I didn't get to know her either because she was packing to leave—for somewhere soon. The third was a tough, scary seventeen year old name Cybil.

Almost one year later, I learned that Cybil was arrested in another institution for *stabbing* a man to death! When I heard that story, I fell to my knees in gratitude—that could have been me!

The three of them were talking loudly and rough-housing while I tried to write a letter to my Mother. They were making me so nervous I felt like pulling my hair out. I tried to ignore them but I couldn't.

Why did I have to listen to this garbage!

And that was my first day.

The next day, my second day there, I decided that I would sit with Bill again in the day room. He really was the only partly normal person I had met in there. We weren't there very long before a social worker walked up to me and told me to follow him to Dr. Locust's office.

As an introduction, this so-called doctor said, "You did something really stupid to get you in here. Are you happy now?"

"I've learned my lesson," I answered, "I'll never do it again."

But he said it was too late for that. He told me I was there forever! And, of course, I reacted just the way he wanted. I went to pieces.

"No!" I shouted, "You can't say that. Don't say that!" I sobbed and sobbed. I kept telling him how sorry I was for attempting to hurt myself. I begged him to let me go home. I told him that I wanted so much to go home.

"That's just tough," he said. "You will be here forever. You will *never* be going home, Rhonda."

Shocked and terrified, I felt like a prisoner. And the more I begged to go home, the more he taunted, "You're *never* going home, Rhonda."

Finally, the social worker came and walked me back to my room. I was shaking and crying and I couldn't understand why I was in this hell. Please God, I prayed, please get me out of here. Please.

> *"Call unto me, I will answer thee and showest thee great and mighty works which thou knowest not." - Jer. 33:3*

In all of my phone calls and letters to my mother I had been telling her how terrible things were here. I told her about the horrible things that I had seen. How there was only one bathroom for ten girls. How I had seen a naked man in the hall yelling at the staff about how hot it was. I told her about the way patients were mistreated by the staff. I told her about the miserable food and how I couldn't eat. And I told her about my traumatic conversation with that sadistic doctor.

Mom naturally relayed all of this horror to my brother, Dean. Dean was stationed in Alaska at this time as soon as he heard about me he phoned me on the pay phone that we all shared on my floor.

The staff supervisor, Martha, stood near me while I was speaking to Dean. She heard me tell him how miserable I was in that place and how upsetting it was meeting with this doctor. At one point, I started to cry because Dean sounded so disappointed and let down by what I had done and where I had ended up. He kept yelling, "Rhonda, you can't take your life. You've committed a sin—a crime! That's why you're in there. I can't believe that you've let this happen to yourself."

AWAKE

The more Dean yelled, the more I cried and it was then that Martha told me that I wouldn't be allowed to get any more calls because they upset me too much. When Dean asked what she had said, I told him and he asked to speak with her. Dean told her that he would definitely be calling me and that I *better* be called to the phone. He also asked her for my doctor's phone number.

The fact that Dean was going to call my doctor really seemed to frighten some of the staff members. They apparently count on patients being drugged and docile. I suppose they weren't accustomed to family members questioning the actions of the staff, much less the doctors.

On my third day, one of my roommates came into the t.v. room where I was sitting. This was Cindy, the forty-something year old who was always with this seventeen year old kid. They both started bragging about something they had done the night before. I wish they hadn't but they described their horrible act in every detail. It seems they ducked behind the Christmas tree, which only hid them partially, and had oral sex.

I was horrified to hear this and immediately phoned my Mother to tell her about it. I know now that I wanted to alarm her as much as possible about my surroundings. As soon as she hung up with me she phoned the hospital's administration and let them know what was going on there. It wasn't long before the social worker came looking for me to tell me that the doctor wanted to see me *again*.

"Why on earth would you tell your Mother everything that you see and hear?"

I was so afraid of him that I immediately apologized and begged his forgiveness. But all he could say was that I wouldn't be allowed to use the telephone any more. And, he said, all of my in-coming calls would be monitored. In addition, I would only be permitted to communicate with my Mother once a week.

Devastated as I was, I knew that those rules would never sit well with my mother and brother. It wasn't long after that second meeting with Doctor Locust that the social worker came and told me that I was to attend a meeting on Friday with my Mother and the doctor. *Please, Mom, bring an attorney!*

Thursday afternoon, I was sitting in the lounge looking at all the stoned patients fighting, slobbering on themselves, or just staring in a daze. *Why doesn't God just let me die quickly? Why can't I get struck by lightning?*

I didn't make or receive any phone calls all that day. When I got up to go to the bathroom, one of the prison-guard-staffers put her hand on my shoulder and pushed me back down. "Where do you think you are going"

"I'm going to the bathroom." I said.

"Oh no you're not." She motioned for another staffer to help her and the two of them *carried* me back to the day room. They told me that if I had to go to the bathroom so badly, I had to use the nearby mens' room.

When I returned from the mens' room, I asked if I could go and take a shower.

"Shut-up and sit down!" was my answer.

Sick and shaking, I returned to my room to write Mom a letter on my bed. My three roommates entered the room at the same time and the mean, scary one said, "Look at the little baby. Why are you crying?"

Between sobs, I said, "Because I don't want to be here. I don't belong here!"

"Well that's just tough," she answered, "and if you don't quit crying, I'll just take you to the bathroom and dunk your head in the toilet." My drowning, she coldly explained, would just be passed-off as another suicide.

At that moment, I knew that I needed to get on my knees and fast! As I prayed, I pleaded, "dear God, if you see this horrible dungeon I'm in, if you know the fear in my heart, then you know that I won't survive this place even a week, let alone ninety days. If you know how scared and sick I am. (I was ill from not eating and the drugs) Please get me out of here. Please, God. If you want me to believe in you, you'll get me out of here."

The next day was Friday and the meeting between my mother and the doctor had only one surprising purpose. He told my Mother that she was free to take me home immediately. No explanation, other than that I had to go immediately unless I was willing to submit to his control as every other patient in the facility did.

Mom and I wasted no time. We were piling all my belongings into my suitcase, terrified that that terrible doctor would change his mind.

As were were heading down the hall, Mom told me that we would have to go back into the doctor's office to get my discharge papers.

No! I didn't want to see that evil man again. I was so afraid he would pull something to keep me locked-up there forever. I would have done anything to avoid that but I knew that Mom was right. We needed those discharge papers.

When we entered his office, Dr. Locust immediately asked if I was ready to leave. *What's the catch*, I thought.

Even Mom was wary of him and kept asking if she could take me out of there immediately.

"That's right," he said. "Just take her out of here right now."

"Are you ready, Rhonda?" Mom said.

I quickly signed my discharge papers with my knees and hands shaking violently. I was feeling horribly sick and the doctor, I'm certain, knew why. He had abruptly cut my eight medications all at once the night before. I was going through a wicked withdrawal. In addition to the fact that I could neither eat nor sleep in that hell hole, the sudden absence of anti-depressants sent me into a tailspin and took more than two and a half weeks for me to overcome.

But since no one had warned us about the effects of the medications being cut so suddenly, we had no idea what was happening to me on that horrible drive home. I became so sick that Mom took me to an emergency room where they explained my condition. I was experiencing withdrawal.

It's criminal the way they pump you full of awful antidepressants. And I have had some of the worst of the worst, Lithium, Prozac, Librium, Anafranil, Tranzene, Artane, Desoreal, Cogentin, Navane, Imiprimine, and Trillafon. While I was an ANI they had me on nine different pills at one time.

But even in frightful sickness that day of my release while we were driving home, it occurred to me that indeed there is a God who heard my prayer. He got me out of that horrid place and I silently told him that I would live for Him from that time on!

"But you are a shield around me O Lord, you bestow glory on me and lift up my head." - Psalms 3:3

INTO THE LIGHT

ONCE I WAS at home with my Mother, I was relieved to have escaped the horrible and hopeless world of depression, medications, doctors, hospitals, loss of privacy, dignity, and freedom. But I knew that I had to learn how to deal with the terrible emptiness that was always with me. I had lost my old life in the car crash. I had no job. My fiancé was gone along with all of my plans and dreams. If I was going to make it, I had to do it alone. Of course my Mother was there for me, but she had a job and a life of her own. Though she had given up a lot, taking care of her head-injured daughter.

Although my short-term memory was now poor, I had vivid memories of my past life. I guess I was lucky that I could remember my life up until the moment of the crash. Some head-injured patients wake up without any memory at all. But being able to remember meant I was always comparing. *I used to speak normally and without hesitation. I used to have a lot of friends. I used to go out all the time. I used to dance and life weights. I used to work and drive a car. I would go on and on.*

I fought hard to stop myself from doing this because I knew I would never allow myself to slip into a depression again and end up in a hospital. That was never going to happen again. Never! Besides I remembered my very sincere prayer back at the institution and how God delivered me from that place.

> *"I love the Lord for He heard my voice, He heard my cry for mercy, because He turned His ear to me I will call on His name as long as I live."* - Psalms 116:1&2

Dan was the last person in my life before my coma so he is the one my mind kept going back to. I had a major struggle just to try not to think about him so much. But I had nothing else in my life. I didn't work. I no longer had my old friends. I was always at home. I was often alone but I knew that I couldn't let myself sink into my old familiar pity party. But I wasn't sure how to accomplish this.

When March came that year, I turned twenty-three. My new friend, Carol and her father came over to our house and helped me celebrate along with my Mother and younger brother, Dom. I had still not heard a word from my so-called dad.

I didn't know it at the time, but there was only one friend that I needed and only one father that I already had. God had protected me during the darkest of times. He was there through everything. And it was because of Him that I was alive and with my family and friends on my twenty-third birthday. But I didn't really understand it yet.

Every night I did thank him for bringing me through everything and I would beg him to send me my heart's companion, my soul mate. *"Please, God, I would say, please, please. I will be forever faithful to you both."*

But I didn't have faith in those days so I thought that I was destined to be sad and lonely forever. I didn't even fully understand yet that all the terrible things that had happened to me had worked for good. That crash took me away from Dan and the destructive and sinful lifestyle I was living. It was His plan for saving me. That's exactly what Barb the nurse back at Harmar Rehab would tell me. "God has allowed this to happen to you for a very special reason, Rhonda, you'll understand one day." But I wasn't ready to know this yet.

Out of her desperation to get me some help and happiness, Mom and her friend drove me all the way to Ohio so that a faith healer could lay hands on me and pray. Of course I didn't go without a fight and when I got there, I was horrible and rude, as I laughed in his face.

Today, however, I am grateful for that trip to Ohio. Mine wasn't an overnight conversion but there were subtle changes in me and my life and I knew it. But it would be another year before I would start attending church regularly.

On a hot summer day in June, I got a phone call from Marilyn, one of the nurses who had been in charge of me when I was back in the coma rooms at Harmarville. She invited me to go to the mall with her. I was thrilled to be going out. So she picked me up and we stopped for something to eat first and then we headed out for a day of shopping. While we were talking, she told me about a nice family she knew who was renting a small house they owned. She said the rent was cheap and that it might be a nice place for me to consider for myself.

Even though I was interested, I told her that I wasn't sure about living alone because I was afraid I would slip back into a depression and end up in the hospital again. Soon tears were soaking my cheeks.

"Rhonda," she said. "You've got to stop feeling sorry for yourself." She knew that inside I was a strong and independent person and I knew it too. I knew that the old Rhonda was trying to come out. I needed independence and freedom. It's what made me who I was and now I had to try to be that person again. I'm sure that that's what brought me out of that coma in a rage. Somewhere in my subconscious, I hated that NG tube, and people turning me over, bathing me, changing my diaper. I'm certain that my very spirit rose up and made me fight my way out of that coma. And I understood that I had to do that again.

That afternoon we rode out to the country where this family lived so that I could talk with them and see the little house they were renting. I did receive money every month and on that very day, I agreed that I would rent this tiny house and pay one hundred and twenty-five dollars a month. Their son even offered to use his truck to help me move my things. He was a nice person and we dated briefly.

It was a big step to take, but Mom and I were driving each other crazy. I was constantly dumping all of my pain and anger on her and I knew that I had to make this move.

The first night in my new house was scary. I wasn't used to living in the country, and I had no car. The family that I rented from lived up over the hill. I did have my dog, but it was still hard.

As always, I knew if I called Dan he'd be in my life again. I could always count on him wanting to see me. But at the same time, I knew with certainty that he was still drinking heavily.

AWAKE

I had always hoped and I suppose, believed that some day Dan would snap out of it and stop drinking. I guess that's why I've been called an idealist, rather than a realist. I now know that this is what always got me into so much trouble.

On August eleventh I called Dan to wish him a happy birthday. We immediately made plans for him to come and visit me. The visit went well. We went out for something to eat and then Dan took me home and left. But the next weekend he was back again—this time drunk as a skunk.

"Baby," he said from the front porch, "what are you doing living way out here without me."

He wanted to come in but I wouldn't let him. Then he started yelling and screaming. But I warned him that if he didn't leave, I would call the police. Finally he threw a beer bottle, shouted some obscenity and skidded away in his car.

Shortly after that, I was watching television and suddenly started gasping for breath. I was panicked so I called my landlady and she drove me to the emergency room. There they told me I was suffering from anxiety and they gave me more pills to take for my nerves.

No wonder I'm having panic attacks with this drunken boyfriend in my life!

I knew I was in a trap with him. We'd just go back and forth forever. I didn't hate him, but I hated what he did. I hated his drinking and he apparently didn't care enough about me to do anything about it. So the cycle continued. Dan would come back or call or I'd call him and we'd see each other for awhile. Then he would show up drunk and violent and I would throw him out. On and on, it went.

Finally I decided that a big part of my problem was loneliness and a big part of my loneliness was living out in the country with no car. Then Mom found a wonderful little apartment back in town just a mile from her house. In late February my dog and I moved into this tiny place. Becky and her boyfriend came and helped me move from the country to the town. My new landlord lived right downstairs and at last I never had to be afraid of anyone breaking in. Now I was close to stores, the bank and beauty shops. Eventually I even found a church I started attending.

"I will give you a new heart and put a new spirit in you."
- Ezekiel 36:26

This is exactly what God had in store for me. It didn't happen over night, it was a process. But before the Holy Spirit nudged me to start attending church, I became entangled in another bad situation. Thinking that I should take control my life, instead of waiting for God, I joined a few dating clubs. None of them led me to anything but tears and problems and one of them arrived in my mail one day. Walking up the stairs to my apartment, I wondered why my phone bill was so thick. When I opened it, I couldn't believe my eyes. My bill was four hundred and forty-four dollars due to all my dating club calls.

I wouldn't ask Mom for the money. I knew that I had gotten myself into this mess and that I alone was responsible. The next day, I drained my savings, which, thank God, was all of five hundred dollars. Again, I learned a very costly lesson.

By the summer of nineteen ninety-two I was determined to have my drivers license renewed and to get a job. Since I had no skills, I cleaned houses for awhile. Mom didn't want me to drive and we argued a lot about that. She told me that because I had a head injury and spent three months in a coma, Harrisburg would never grant me another drivers license. She said that if I ever tried to drive again I would be arrested. She insisted that I should *never* drive again. I, however, was just as insistent that I *would* drive again. True to form, her telling me that I absolutely could not do something made me try even harder to do it.

I knew that I would have no future if I didn't drive. I'd never get a job and if I never got a job and didn't ever drive, who would want me? What would happen to me? It was bad enough that Mom told me that it was too dangerous for me to ever have children because of my VP shunt. How could I ever find someone to love me. How would I ever have a life?

First I phoned Harmarville Rehabilitation I was not only determined to drive but to do it legally. It took about a million calls and an incredible amount of red tape. But finally, after

AWAKE

about two months of work, I got authorization to allow me to begin drivers training. For the first time in a very long time, I was excited.

I began drivers training, working with two different teachers. One put me at ease and gave me confidence but the other made me uneasy. But I was learning to deal with difficult people and I completed my lessons and did fairly well.

But when the time came to take my drivers test, I was a wreck. I couldn't sleep the night before. All through those long, lonely hours, I prayed and worried. My friend, Carol and I had discussed how I had to be careful not to become emotional or flip out regardless of how I did on the test. We knew that they would be watching my reactions and how I handled myself.

I got the results of my test over the phone from the instructor I thought was the nice one. I had failed the test. I fought back a river of tears as I heard their decision. When I hung-up, I vented my emotions by tossing all of the car advertisements I had been collecting and got back to walking everywhere I had to go.

I might not have a job or a car but I did have a lot a people who cared about me and my lack of a social life. And did they ever try to help. My landlady fixed me up with a guy she knew, her son fixed me up with another one, my friend Carol fixed me up, even my mom fixed me up with a young man from work. They were all very nice but they were not God's choice for me.

Though Carol was the best sounding board for my depression and loneliness, there were times when I'd sink low enough to call Dan crying the blues. If I caught him on a good day, talking with him wouldn't be too bad. But if he happened to be drunk or hung over, I would get an earful of his cursing misery. I swear the devil was talking through him. He always told me that he'd kill me before he'd let anyone else have me.

But I was not alone in this and slowly God gave me the strength to stop making those destructive calls. As I pulled farther and farther away from Dan, I was drawn closer to God and as if that wasn't enough, God gave me confirmation of his presence in my life.

"Be strong in the Lord and in the power of His might."
- Eph: 6:10

It happened one warm day when I was in my apartment looking through a magazine from church. Suddenly I was looking at a picture that was identical to a vision I had had when I was about ten years old. My mother, brother, and I had been at my grandmother's house. While she and my grandmother visited, Dom and I had been playing outside where Mom could see us through the window. We had been running up and down these really big hills of dirt, going as fast as we could. But once, just as I reached the top of a hill, I caught a glimpse of something in the sky and this something was a hand. It wasn't a cloud that looked like a hand, nor was it a plane. It was a huge hand that was in a cupped position.

I don't know how but I somehow knew that I was seeing something holy and wonderful. But I also knew not to share this with too many people because I wouldn't be believed.

"See, I have engraved you on the palms of my hands."
- Is.49:16

That day when I found the picture in the magazine that looked like my vision, I once again had that rock-solid certainty that this was God's way of saying, "Rhonda, I will be carrying you through. Just hang in there and don't give up."

But still I had more to go through and more to learn. I made a lot of mistakes during this time.

In the meantime, I had a frightening experience one night at about eleven when there was a knock at my door. Foolishly, I opened it and a drunk Dan pushed his way in and started slamming me around.

"Get out, Dan," I screamed. "I don't want you here. I can't stand how bad you stink!" He responded by putting his hands around my throat—tighter and tighter. I could barely breathe. But somehow I managed to kick him away and run upstairs where I called the police. "The cops are coming for you, Dan. Get out now!"

I screamed down the stairs. But he only laughed and staggered his way up stairs.

"I know you didn't call the police, Baby."

But the police were there in no time and Dan was hauled out of the house in handcuffs and thrown in jail for the night. Once out, he continued to call me when he was drunk, blaming me for all his troubles.

Since I was unable to drive, I would take long walks and one day while walking, I wandered into a church. (This was about a year after the faith healer prayed for me.) I didn't know anyone who went to this church but something made me go in. Soon, I was going to that church on a regular basis. But since I was only at the beginning of my healing, I still had some more mistakes to make—like still believing that I could change Dan.

I actually convinced him once to accompany me to church. What a mistake that was! The whole hour and a half that we were there, he kept checking the time and couldn't wait to leave. All through the service he kept asking me if I would go with him for a drink when we got out.

"Can't you even stop drinking on a Sunday, Dan?"

"Resist the devil and he will flee from you!"
- James 4:7

Ye shall know the truth and the truth will make you free."
- John 8:32

Why couldn't I accept that Dan wasn't going to quit drinking for me, himself, or anyone. He thought going out drinking with him was the very least I could do since he sat through a church service with me. The evening ended, as usual, in a fight with me going home alone in tears. But as I was crying myself to sleep that night, I prayed and begged God to bring me a good man. Little did I know that that special person God had picked out for me was also alone and praying at the very same time.

We only think that we're clever enough to arrange our lives

but I'm here to tell you that it can't be be done. Leave everything to God and His plan, in His good time will be the very best for you—better than you can ever imagine.

Week after week I returned to that church and didn't know why. But God still had more lessons for me to learn before my life would truly change.

> *"Therefore, if any man be in Christ, he is a new creature, the old things have passed away, behold new things have come."* - II. Cor. 5:17

I had been attending the church for a few months when a travelling evangelist came to do some services. After the first service, he approached me and told me that he had noticed me. He also told me that he felt that I was a special person and he hoped that I would continue to come to hear him speak.

Walking home that night, I was flattered and pleased by his reaction to me. But the next day, I was surprised to get a call from him. He told me that he had gotten my phone number from the church bulletin where I had advertised for house cleaning jobs. He asked if I lived with my parents and wanted to know if he could call me later that night. I told him he could but I was surprised when he did phone back after ten that night. Though his conversation was much too personal for a so-called man of God, I still wasn't quite clear in my assessment of him. After all, everyone in this church thought the world of him. How could he be anything but what he represented. I continued to attend his services and during one of them, I was saved and led to the Lord by him.

> *"He which hath begun a good work in you will perform it until the day of Jesus Christ."* - Phil 1:6

But his late night calls continued and in every one he got bolder and bolder. By now it was clear to me that he thought that since I had had a brain injury, that he could take advantage of me. Though we were never alone together, he even admitted to me that he didn't know if he could control himself in such a situation with me.

AWAKE

At the end of the week, I was thankful when he left town. His behavior had made me doubt this church and the people in it. But something kept me going back in spite of my bad experience with the evangelist. I never told anyone but my friend, Carol about my experience since I felt they would never believe me over him. So I just kept quiet and kept attending services.

I now know that whatever demons he had to battle, whatever character flaws he may have had, this man had led me to salvation and my salvation was real and true. And nothing and no one can change that.

> *"For by grace you are saved through faith and not of yourselves, it is the gift of God." - Eph. 2:8*

One morning at the close of services in October of nineteen ninety-three, as I was heading down the aisle toward the door, I saw a man standing at the back. I thought this man might know my friend, Carol since I knew that they both attended the same Christian center. When I approached him, I introduced myself and asked him about Carol. It turned out that he didn't know her but he was happy, it seemed, to know me, and he told me that his name was Carl.

I had seen Carl in church from time to time. He was always alone but I think that I always assumed that he, like everyone else, had a wife at home. I was always alone in church too, but I sat in the front and Carl was always in a back pew. We had had contact briefly once before though. As had happened at so many services, I had been sobbing and as I was leaving, still teary and red-eyed, he approached me and gave me a hug saying, "Hang in there. Everything will be okay."

> *"The things you have learned and received in me, practice these things and the God of peace shall always be with you." - Phil. 4:9*

On that October day, Carl nearly let me get out of the church doors before he worked up the nerve to ask me to go and have lunch with him. That lunch lasted for three hours as we talked, laughed, and got to know each other. At first I just thought we were two lonely people keeping each other company for awhile. He was, after all, several years my senior. So, I thought, this will be a great friendship. But very quickly I began to realize that Carl was the most gentle, caring, loving, faithful, and devoted man I had ever met. Incredibly God had sent me exactly what I had prayed for—a companion and soul mate—someone who would care for me as though God had said, "Carl, I have someone picked out for you who needs you to shower her with love and attention to make her feel special and loved."

"I will extol the Lord at all times, His praise will always be on my lips." - Psalms 34:1

Carl proposed to me a little more than two years after our first date. It was Valentines Day and he took me to The Top of the Triangle Restaurant overlooking downtown Pittsburgh. There were roses, chocolates, and even a violin being played when he asked me to marry him and offered me a dazzling ring.

"He will bless those who fear the Lord, the small together with the great." - Psalms 115:13

On July twentieth, nineteen ninety-six, Carl and I stood before God and in the presence of our family and friends and were united in holy matrimony. Carol was thrilled to be our maid of honor. It was all my dreams coming true on one beautiful, shining summer day. Me in a beautiful, flowing white gown and Carl, so handsome in white tails. And together, God and Carl even put together the kind of honeymoon cruise that I never could have imagined would have happened to me.

One of the most important things Carl taught me through his faith is "Seek first His kingdom and His righteousness, all these things shall be added unto you." - Matthew 6:33

Since meeting and falling in love, the hymn "Isn't It

Amazing" always meant a great deal to Carl and me. We decided that it would be a perfect touch if we sang that hymn to each other at our wedding. Though we practiced singing, I was worried that even with the use of a microphone, I wouldn't be heard since my injury had caused the volume of my voice to be lower. But God took care of everything that day and we did beautifully. And, incredibly, I got through that magnificent ceremony without shedding a single tear.

"The Lord will give strength to His people, the Lord will bless His people with peace." - Psalms 29:11

So I was able to come from the jaws of death, from the darkness of brain damage, depression, loneliness and despair into the glorious light of God's love showered on me through the love of my husband. And how that love changed me. I used to be nervous, worried, and jealous of other people. I used to compare myself to other people. I wanted the happiness they had. And now I have learned that the way to that kind of happiness is through God—putting all of your trust in Him as the bible says, *"Trust in the Lord with all your heart, and do not lean on your own understanding. In all your ways acknowledge Him, and He will make your paths straight." - Proverbs 3:5&6*

Every bit of this is true and this as well,

"The end of a thing is better than the beginning thereof and the patient in spirit is better than the proud in spirit."
- Ecc. 7:8

Mom, Carl, me, and Carol, Christmas, 1993.

Carl and me at Kennywood, 1994.

Our romantic proposal dinner at the Top of the Triangle Restaurant in Pittsburgh, February, 1995.

An evening out on the Gateway Clipper. Carl and I were happily engaged and planning our wedding.

Celebrating New Years Eve, 1995.
So much to look forward to in the coming year.

Me with my precious Daisy Mae, 1996.
"Blessed are the pure in heart, for they shall see God."
– Matthew 5:8

AWAKE

"What God has joined together, Let no man separate."
— Matthew 19-6

Rhonda R. Durand

God's grace has me glowing!

Sweeter than the cake, this is the man I've been praying for.

"God sets the lonely in families." – PS. 68:6

Dom sharing in Rhonda's happiness.

A new beginning with Mom, Grandma, and my handsome hubby.

Our wonderful journey begins.

The lord, he has done great things.

Epilogue

FROM THAT SUNDAY afternoon in 1993, Carl and I began to see how God orchestrated our coming together—our church-going, our first words to each other, the three-hour lunch date, our friendship, and our blessed, beautiful wedding day.

I understand now why God allowed the accident to happen. I understand the depression that controlled my thinking and the years of recovery. God in His sovereignty permitted the lesser pain of the accident to persuade me to change the dangerous lifestyle I was living.

I have in no way cheated death for I know that I will one day die. I have an appointed time and as God's word says, *"And in as much as it is appointed unto man to die, but after this comes judgement." - Hebrews. 9:27* Are you ready for judgement? God will have the final say. He will punish the wicked, He will reward those who trust in Him. But God demonstrates His love toward us in that *"while we were yet sinners, christ died for us." - Romans 5-8*

With that assurance, this apparent injustice is nothing, knowing, as I do, that God is always in control. I can face my future appointment with death knowing that the shed blood of Jesus Christ my savior will reconcile me to a Holy God.

> *"Unless a man is born again, he cannot see the Kingdom of God.* - John 3:3

Most recently, I began working with elementary school students. From my very first day and every day since, there has been this beautiful little girl who comes to me to embrace me with very big, tight hugs. When I looked down and asked her her name, she smiled at me and said "Angel. My name is Angel."

To me, it was a kind of confirmation of the conversation my Mom had in the restroom with the young woman who confidently insisted that I would survive.

Our new love, the beautiful Rumba Reneé.

*"For you O Lord have delivered my soul from death,
my eyes from tears, my feet from stumbling,
that I may walk before the Lord in the land of the living."
- Psalms 116:8&9*

A Simple Plan of Salvation

CONFESSING TO GOD that I am a hopeless sinner and believing in my heart that Jesus Christ died for my sins on the cross and was raised for my justification.
 I do now receive and confess Him as my personal savior. Amen.

1992 I received salvation
1993 I met Carl
1996 Carl and I married
1997 We were blessed with appearances on six Christian television programs and gave twelve church testimonials
 1998 We lost our beloved Daisy Mae and nine months later we adopted our beautiful Rumba Reneé.
2002 I got back to work after fifteen years of unemployment. Dan passes away at age 37.
2004 I got a book contract!
2005 We moved, God answering exactly as to selling our home and providing us with another home that is perfect for us. Carl and I look forward to another year filled with God's peace and blessings.
2006 Carl and I will renew our vows for our 10th anniversary.

 "Truly I say to you unless you are converted and become like children you shall not enter into the kingdom of heaven."
— Matthew 18:3

 Each and every time we encounter a trial, God is right by our side to see us through.
 Are you ready for judgement?